Mobile Persuasion:
20 Perspectives
on the
Future of Behavior Change

Mobile Persuasion:
20 Perspectives
on the
Future of Behavior Change

Edited by

B.J. Fogg, Ph.D.
and
Dean Eckles

Persuasive Technology Lab
Stanford University

Published by
Stanford Captology Media

Stanford, California

For more information, please contact:
Stanford Captology Media
Stanford University
122 Cordura Hall
Palo Alto, California 94305
Or send an email to mobilepersuasion@csli.stanford.edu

ISBN 978-0-9795025-2-1

Table of Contents

Design Insights _____

The Bigger Picture _____

We still can't explain why, but something changed in 2006. People in the U.S. suddenly became interested in mobile phones as platforms for persuasion. Our evidence for this change is limited, but we find it compelling: In early 2005 our Persuasive Technology Lab at Stanford University blogged about hosting a conference on mobile persuasion. We got almost no response. Our lab team sat back and scratched our collective heads: "Why aren't people interested in this topic?" we wondered. We didn't have the answer.

Our lab had been investigating mobile persuasion since 2001. The more we researched this topic, the more we were intrigued. However, our blog post in 2005 received almost no interest. So we cancelled our plans for the event, and we continued our own research into mobile persuasion, which at that point was our lab's primary focus in captology.

Eighteen months later, in July 2006, we made a similar announcement. We blogged about hosting a conference on mobile persuasion: "Is anyone interested?" Our second announcement was similar to the first one, and we were expecting the response to be cold again.

But we were wrong.

In 2006 the response was hot. In fact, it was so hot that we had to postpone the event five months so we could find a larger venue and plan for a crowd.

Mobile Persuasion 2007 sold out to 250 participants. A couple dozen people who learned about the event late showed up without registration and crashed the party. We can't really blame the crashers. This was a unique gathering.

In one day we heard from over 30 speakers from a variety of backgrounds. From anthropologists to game designers to trend watchers, each presented a different piece of the mobile persuasion puzzle. By design, the speakers focused on the psychological aspects of mobile persuasion. As we listened and talked, we tried to see the patterns and the bigger picture. We all learned a lot about the realities of mobile persuasion, and the potential.

Our Stanford lab wanted to share these ideas beyond the event, so we invited several Mobile Persuasion 2007 speakers to share their perspectives in print. And that's what led to this book.

You'll notice that our title emphasizes behavior change. We admit this is a biased view of persuasion, a concept that usually means changing attitudes and opinions. But we believe that changing behaviors is more important. Today's political, social, and environmental problems are not going to be solved with mass changes in opinion. We need mass changes in behavior. In our view that's what mobile persuasion is all about.

As editors, we've given the authors lots of freedom. You'll find a wide range of approaches, writing styles, and worldviews. We encourage you to think of each chapter as a different person's opinion. Please don't expect all the ideas to cohere into a tidy worldview of mobile persuasion; our understanding of this emerging domain is too limited today.

We feel fortunate to bring together, for the first time, a variety of experts who share insight into how mobile phones will be the channel for changing people's behaviors in the future. We've organized the chapters to tell something of a story: What's possible today, what's coming next, what's on the edge, and how all of this will change our culture deeply.

The last chapter in this book, Perspective #20, is something of a surprise. It's in this chapter that we invite you to share your views on mobile persuasion by going to www.MobilePersuasion.com. At this website you'll find new insights from others who have read this book. You can contribute your own perspective in text, pictures, or video.

By creating a book with an open chapter, we are saying two things: First, we recognize that we don't have all the answers about mobile persuasion. Second, we believe there are many people who can contribute to our conversation online and in future gatherings and publications.

You're not arriving late to the mobile persuasion party. Not at all. We hope we've made it clear that this book is not the final word on the subject. Quite the opposite: We see this book as the official beginning of the conversation. What you'll find here are the first few comments in a larger, ongoing dialogue. So you're not late. You're arriving at the party in good time. As such, we invite you to join us and help to shape the future.

Your hosts,

B.J. Fogg, Ph.D.
Dean Eckles

Persuasive Technology Lab
Stanford University

Overview

Perspective 1

The Future of Persuasion is Mobile

B.J. Fogg, Persuasive Technology Lab, Stanford University

I believe mobile phones will soon become the most important platform for changing human behavior. Within 15 years, no other medium—TV, word of mouth, the web—will be more effective at changing what we humans believe and what we do.

We are on the cusp of a persuasion revolution. Think down the road 15 years and imagine how this will work. Through mobile technology, insurance companies will motivate us to exercise, governments will advocate energy conservation, charities will persuade us to donate time, and suitors will win the hearts of their beloveds. Nothing can stop this revolution.

I see three reasons that mobile phones will rule the persuasion universe. To make these reasons memorable, I propose three metaphors: a heart (we love our mobile phones), a wristwatch (they are with us always), and a magic wand (these devices have many capabilities).

First Comes Love . . .

Has there ever been a technology more personal and more loved than the mobile phone? Despite the aggravation they sometimes cause, we are so smitten by these little objects that we feel lost without them. Just think about your own life: If you go out for the evening and forget your phone at home, you will probably feel anxious. You won't feel completely whole, entirely yourself. Like the love of your life, the mobile phone completes you. What else indicates love if it's not yearning for the object of desire when we're apart?

And why shouldn't we be enamored? The connectivity and capability these devices offer is hard not to love. And the sales figures show how we are responding globally. Rich or poor, young or old, educated or not—everyone wants a mobile phone.

In some ways, we don't merely adopt mobile devices; we marry them. We usually spend more time with our mobile phones than with our spouses or partners. Just count up the hours and compare. On the flip side, nothing else in the world—not even our favorite t-shirt—spends more time in our presence. For this reason alone, those of us who design mobile interactions need to view the mobile–human relationship as the most personal, intensive, and lasting of all relationships.

> Emotions and behavior change are linked. When we feel trust, competence, and delight, we open ourselves to be more flexible, to try out new behaviors.

We may not get our cues from Dr. Phil, Dr. Laura, or Dr. Ruth, but perhaps we should take the love and marriage metaphor seriously. The best interactions in a marriage will create feelings of trust, competence, and delight. As mobile designers, this should be our goal. The interactions we design should give people these same positive feelings. Emotions and behavior change are linked. When we feel trust, competence, and delight, we open ourselves to be more flexible, to try out new behaviors.

Always by My Side . . .

The second reason mobile phones will be the leading platform for persuasion has to do with how they travel with us most everywhere. They are always by our side, or at least near at hand. The mobile technology is with us as we live our lives—seeking information, making decisions, taking action, regretting our misdeeds. The mobile phone sees all.

In my book *Persuasive Technology,* I explained how mobile phones will eventually leverage the Greek concept of *kairos*—attempting to persuade at the right time. This still holds true; nothing is better positioned in our lives to intervene at the opportune moment. But now I'm ready to go beyond kairos and explain three ways that the mobile phone's omnipresence becomes persuasive. Instead of using Greek abstractions, I'll describe three persuasive roles that the mobile phone can play: concierge, coach, and court jester. As far as I can tell, all the examples in this book fit into one of these categories.

My Concierge

The omnipresent mobile phone can act as a virtual concierge. When we need information or guidance, we can turn to the device for answers. The mobile phone can respond with help in our moment of need. And like a real concierge, the information our mobile phone provides—and the experience of presenting the information—can be designed to influence us.

Consider a personal example: On a recent trip to Kauai, I asked the hotel concierge to recommend a healthy restaurant for dinner. She offered a name and handed me a map. The dinner was good, but I have to wonder: Was her suggestion biased? Like a real-world concierge, a mobile concierge can influence, even manipulate, what we think and do. Let's hope it's for the better.

> **The mobile phone can respond with help in our moment of need. And like a real concierge, the information our mobile phone provides can be designed to influence us.**

My Coach

The next role for mobile persuasion is coach. The mobile phone can track our goals and our context. When the time is right, this mobile coach can prompt us to take action. For example, on my mom's birthday, the phone can prompt me to phone her in the morning. Or when I'm leaving for vacation, the mobile coach could prompt me to turn off all my computers. The role of concierge and coach are different: I go to the concierge for help; the coach comes to me. In later chapters of this book you'll see examples of both.

My Court Jester

The third role for mobile persuasion is court jester, which may be the most interesting role of all. Like court jesters of old, the mobile phone can amuse us with games, fun information, or flirty social interactions. Sometimes we call for the court jester when we're bored. Other times, we want to distract ourselves from life's routines.

While we're having fun, it's easy to forget that the court jester can be sneaky. He can broach topics no one else dares and can persuade us when we least expect it. Consider how some comedians today talk about social and political issues in ways that "serious" news cannot. Likewise, amusement on mobile technology can be an effective vehicle for persuasion.

The Magic Wand . . .

Now to my third reason: The mobile phone will become the dominant persuasion channel because of its capabilities. I can think of no technology more enchanting or more personally empowering. With the simplest of mobile phones, I can talk with almost anyone in the world. I can float down a river in California and chat with a friend on safari in Africa. No special training required. To me, that's magic.

With a more sophisticated phone in hand, I could use the internet capabilities to launch a new business or to organize a political movement. The world has never seen such power in such a small package. The idea of accomplishing so much, so conveniently, was once a fantasy; now it's a reality.

We can harness these powers to change human behavior. On one hand, we could use our skills to control other people. But what interests me more is on the other hand—how the mobile platform can help motivate people to achieve their own personal goals. I believe this approach to mobile persuasion is most fitting and natural: We choose our own goals, we pick our own paths, and our mobile devices help us succeed, like a magic wand in our service.

> I believe this approach to mobile persuasion is most fitting and natural: We choose our own goals, we pick our own paths, and our mobile devices help us succeed, like a magic wand in our service.

Other chapters in this book give insight into how mobile persuasion will work. You'll see how mobile text, audio, and video can influence people at the right time and place. You'll learn about examples of interactive reminders, rewards, and progress tracking. You'll read how mobile games change our worldview and, eventually, our behaviors. You'll also see how the phone can connect us to supportive peers or expert advisors.

Web 2.0 Is a Dress Rehearsal

The growing capabilities of the mobile platform will lead to new persuasive services that we can't yet predict. But we can make some guesses about how mobile technology will affect existing internet services, what's being called "Web 2.0" today. These new forms of online media and social interaction have blossomed in part because they've figured out how to persuade users to perform target behaviors—to register for the service, upload content, invite friends to join, and so on. If companies like Flickr and Digg didn't persuade people effectively, they would have failed.

Despite the success of such services on the personal computer, I believe they are merely a dress rehearsal. Once we resolve input and output issues for mobile devices (and solve some industry coordination problems), then the dress rehearsal will end for Web 2.0 services and the real show will begin, on the mobile stage.

Virtually all of today's successful Web 2.0 services will get better—more useful, more fun, more persuasive—when people can access the most compelling aspects of these services from a mobile device. For instance, Mobile Digg can give you the most interesting stories while you ride the train. Mobile Flickr can make it easier for people to post comments about your photos.

> **Virtually all of today's successful Web 2.0 services will get better—more useful, more fun, more persuasive—when people can access the most compelling aspects of these services from a mobile device.**

The convenience of mobile access makes it easier for Web 2.0 services to motivate people to perform the critical target behaviors. For example, a mobile handset makes it more convenient to rate stories in Digg, comment on photos in Flickr, or introduce business colleagues using LinkedIn. We could do these activities from almost anywhere at any time. As a result, those target behaviors will happen more often, and this increase will make the service better for everyone.

But here's the hard part: To succeed at this next level, each Web 2.0 service first must understand the compelling essence of their user experience (for example, in Flickr, the magic happens when people comment on your photos). Next, companies need to figure out how to deliver that core experience via mobile devices. If they fail to deliver the essence—the magic—the mobile service will fail.

Mobile Technology Will Bias Our Perceptions

Not every service will migrate to mobile from the web. But mobile offers some unique opportunities, especially when it comes to what I call "technology-enhanced social interactions." While this new category exists on the desktop (think Facebook or SecondLife), persuasion becomes more relevant when mobile devices enhance our social interactions.

Consider the example of road rage. If your mobile device could help you better understand the distracted driver in front of you (e.g., her child has just been injured at school) your response to the erratic driving would be more patient. Of course, this example is hypothetical. My point is that mobile technology can layer information into our moment-by-moment lives in a way that changes our behavior. For this reason I'm intrigued with augmented reality, which is explored later in this book. The big

> **Mobile technology can layer information into our moment-by-moment lives in a way that changes our behavior.**

question for me is, Who controls what gets added to your world? Those who control the augmentation are those who shape our perceptions and ultimately control our behaviors.

So Much To Gain; So Much To Lose

As you go about your life, think about the impact of picking up your mobile phone and putting that small wonder in your pack, purse, or pocket. With this simple act, you are changing the world. You, along with billions of others, are promoting a revolution in persuasion.

What will this revolution do for you? What do you *want* it to do for you?

With the power of mobile persuasion in your hand, will you be motivated to strengthen your relationships? To get more physically fit? To conserve Earth's resources? Will you be persuaded to pursue a new hobby? Volunteer in your community? Vote for honest and capable leaders who seek global harmony? The possibilities are nearly endless.

I'm convinced that the mobile phone will be the most powerful and amazing of our human creations. But I'm not convinced we will ultimately use the power of mobile persuasion for good purposes. I hope we do. In my lab at Stanford University we're trying to do our part to ensure that. By focusing our research on mobile persuasion, by organizing conferences, creating curricula, and even producing this book, we intend to help put mobile persuasion on a good path. We invite collaborations. When many of us make a sustained effort in the right direction, the odds for success get better. Working together we can shape the persuasion revolution so that it enhances the quality of life for individuals, communities, and society.

About the Author

Dr. B.J. Fogg was awarded Stanford University's Maccoby Prize in 1998 for four years of experimental research on how computers can change people's attitudes and behaviors. He then founded the Stanford Persuasive Technology Lab, where he directs research and design related to mobile persuasion. Most years he teaches courses in captology for two Stanford departments. He also devotes time to industry projects and innovations, which has led to nine patents and seven patents pending. B.J. is the author of *Persuasive Technology: Using Computers to Change What We Think and Do.*

Perspective 2

Using Technology to Promote Youth Sexual Health

Deb Levine
Executive Director, ISIS (Internet Sexuality Information Services, Inc.)

I've been working on the internet in the field of sexual health and relationships for more than a decade now, starting with the development of Columbia University's award-winning, question-and-answer service, Go Ask Alice (www.goaskalice.columbia.edu). While working at Columbia as a health educator, it became clear that students were learning in a different way than the adult professionals had. Lecture-style teaching didn't have much of an impact, unless there was an imminent exam.

In 1993, campuses were being wired with high-speed cables, and students were taking advantage of free email accounts and network services. It didn't take a rocket scientist to figure out that providing health information via these network services would reach a larger audience than mandatory late night group talks in the dorms. In 2001, after spending a few years consulting in the health and technology field, I founded Internet Sexuality Information Services, Inc. (ISIS), www.isis-inc.org, a non-profit organization dedicated to using technology for sexual health promotion and disease prevention. We are dedicated to enhancing sexual communication and knowledge for all populations by any means necessary. These days, that extends to the mobile sector as well as the internet, print, and face-to-face dialogue.

An Urgent Need for Education

Research shows that 44% of U.S. high school youth have had sex, and 14% report four or more lifetime sex partners. Unfortunately, only 62% of youth reported using a condom the last time they had sex. With over 40 million human immunodeficiency virus (HIV) infections worldwide and half of new infections occurring in people under the age of 24, there is an urgent need to develop new and effective sex education and HIV prevention approaches.

There is also an urgent need to address a little known risk of teen relationships—dating violence, which in today's teen population, is happening in a technologically savvy way. A recent study[1] found that 20%–30% of teens who had been in relationships said their partner had constantly checked in on them, had harassed or insulted them, or had made unwanted requests for sexual activity, all via cell phones or text messages. One out of four reported hourly contact with a dating partner between midnight and 5:00 a.m.—in some cases, 30 times per hour. And one out of ten had received physical threats electronically.

> There is an urgent need to develop new and effective sex education and HIV prevention approaches.

A much smaller percentage of parents reported that their teens had had such experiences—meaning that this type of abuse can go undetected, sometimes causing breakdowns or escalations in abuse or violence that are seemingly unprecipitated. This all points to an urgent need to reach youth with critical health information about sexuality and relationships in a manner with which they are comfortable and familiar, in a way that is consistent with youth culture.

Youth, Sex and Technology

Young people receive information in a different way than people over 30: They only "hear" information that is directly relevant to their lives at a particular moment. This puts our traditional disease- and violence-prevention efforts at odds with teenagers' real lives.

How can we persuade youth to care about developing sexual health and positive relationships in the context of the fast pace and changing nature of their lives? There has always been a simple answer: By meeting them where they're at. Professionals must provide the information young people want, when and how they want it. We must reach young people with information

> We must reach young people with information that will empower them to make key decisions at a time and in a manner with which they are familiar.

that will empower them to make key decisions at a time and in a manner with which they are familiar.

To learn how young people send and receive information, visit any high school, mall, or video arcade. There you will see that most youth have mobile phones and use them to "thumb text" messages to their friends during the course of their regular activities. Texting allows youth to use mobile phones for private communication.

> Technology allows us to reach young people with 24-hour-a-day, internet access and mobile phone coverage, so that any given moment becomes a teachable one.

Health professionals who work with teens can take advantage of this phenomenon. Technology allows us to reach young people with 24-hour-a-day internet access and mobile phone coverage, so that any given moment becomes a teachable one. Whether a young person is deciding to have sex for the first time, or if a condom just broke, whether a boyfriend is texting a break-up or a girlfriend is cyber-stalking, relevant information and referrals can be conveyed via mobile phones in a personal, private way at the moment when a teen needs them most.

Mobile Solution: The SexINFO Service

In 2006, ISIS developed a pilot, text-messaging program with funding from the San Francisco Department of Public Health. The service, called SexINFO, is a sexual health service for youth that is accessible via mobile phones. The service is "opt-in," whereby the user texts the word "SEXINFO" to short code 61827, to reach a directory of 11 questions, with codes instructing the user to text for example, "A1 if the condom broke," "B2 if u think ur pregnant," "D4 if someone's hurting u," or "F8 if he or she's cheating on u." All answers include basic support information and referrals to local in-person resources (see Figure 1.) There is a companion website, www.sextext.org, where parents and others can view the messages available to youth via their phones.

"**A1**" if ur condom broke
A1 SEXINFO: u may b at risk 4 STDs+HIV women can also be prgnant SouthEast Keith@Armstrong 671-7000 M–F8–5, W8–12. City Clinic 356 7th St 487-5500 MWF 8–4 TuTh 1–4

"**B2**" if u think ur pregnant
B2 SEXINFO: it's ur choice what 2 do testing+morningafterpill up to 5 days aftr sex New Generations WF 9–3:30;502-8336;625 Portr Healing Arts 5190 Third TTH 1–4

"**C3**" to find out about STDs
C3 SEXINFO: if u hve sex, u can get an STD + not know it. Chlamydia, gonorrhea=no symptoms most of the time Dropin get checked FREE 356 7th St. 8–4 MWF, 1–4 TuTh

"**D4**" to find out about HIV
D4 SEXINFO: u can get HIV from sex, blood, or sharing needles w/someone infected free RAPID HIV tests Larkin 673-0911 x259 M–F 2–4:30; HipHop 337-4719 MTh 1–5

"**E5**" if u need 2 talk now
E5 SEXINFO: if ur feeling down, like the world sucks, like u wanna xcape ur life, call SF Suicide Prvntion 2 talk 781-0500 24/7 not just 4 suicide

"**F6**" if she or he's cheating on u
F6 SEXINFO: if u think s/he's cheating on u, get a checkup 2day STDs can go backnforth most times there's no symptoms drop-in City Clinic 356 7th St 487-5500

"**F8**" if ur not sure u want to have sex
F8 SEXINFO: it's ur choice to have sex or not get informed before u decide Balboa/1000 Cayuga469-4512; 9-4 M-F; Cole St Clinic 555 Cole St dropin Th 2-6; 751-8181

© 2007 isis-inc.org

Figure 1. SexINFO is a mobile-based sexual health service targeted to young people. The service takes advantage of the popularity of text messaging as a primary means of communication among youth.

What We Have Learned

Health and counseling professionals do not need to be technically savvy to implement mobile-based solutions that will reach and motivate young people. The same tools and best practices used in traditional informational and prevention programs for youth can be applied to developing mobile solutions. We offer the following advice on how to get started, based on what we've learned from our experience with SexINFO:

1) **Get familiar with your mobile phone.** At ISIS, we all changed our text messaging plans to UNLIMITED and started texting everyone we know, including each other across the office, just to familiarize ourselves with the

experience of texting. (When I was at one San Francisco clinic, a doctor called me into an exam room, closed the door, and asked me to show him what the heck to do.)

2) **Practice writing succinctly.** We started working in Microsoft Word files, writing out answers to the most commonly asked sex questions, then condensing the answers to a maximum of 160 characters, including spaces.

3) **Know your community.** We had a hunch that the web was "over" and that text messaging was the "new, new thing." But not until we sat down with young people did we hear the real scoop about how they were using their phones. And oh my, did we hear a lot!

4) **Hire consultants.** We're health educators and public health professionals—content experts, not technologists. Once we realized that we didn't need to be engineers, it was easier to apply our skills to hire good engineers to assist us in setting up the SexINFO service.

4) **Plan Ahead.** Since ISIS is always innovating, we've learned that it's important to make sure there's enough funding to support a new service. That includes funds to create a strong marketing program that will attract a critical mass to use the service, as well as funds to collect data to evaluate the service after it has been in use for a reasonable period of time.

Sample Youth Comments about SexINFO

"A lot of teenagers don't go to clinics, and we're afraid to ask questions. Text messaging, it's no one's business but yours. So you don't have to talk to someone face to face if you think you're pregnant or a condom broke. You don't have to feel embarrassed or humiliated."—*Michelle*

"I used to get my sex education from a radio program for young people. But now that I'm older, I'm learning most of what I know about sex from 'experience and friends.' I'm on my cell phone all the time, so it's pretty cool that now I can send a text message for safer sex advice."—*Mattie*

"I think kids will use it. I send 'about 100' text messages a day now." — *Alex*

"I learned about sex from Judy Blume's Forever and the girlie mags the kids down the street stole out of their dad's closet. I can think of a lot of mistakes I would have avoided if I'd had access to a program like SexInfo."—*John*

Adapting to a Changing World

Keeping up with youth culture and changing technology is no easy feat for professionals who must stay on top of clinical and diagnostic updates in their field as well. But ignoring the changing world of technology does a disservice to our youth. Working together with youth in our communities, we can use new media tools to educate, inform, and empower young people to take more responsibility for maintaining their sexual health.

End Notes

[1] The study was commissioned by Liz Claiborne, Inc. and conducted by Teenage Research Unlimited.

[2] Standard messaging rates apply.

About the Author

Deb Levine has been working professionally on the internet for more than 12 years. At Columbia University, she designed an award-winning online sexual health Q&A service, Go Ask Alice! She wrote a sex advice column, Ask Delilah, for AOL and Time-Warner, and the Sexuality blog on Yahoo! Health. Deb is an adjunct at San Francisco State University and the author of *The Joy of Cybersex: A Guide for Creative Lovers* (Ballantine 1998), as well as numerous academic papers. Internet Sexuality Information Services (ISIS), is a 501(c)(3) organization that uses technology for sexual-health promotion and disease prevention.

Perspective 3

MyFoodPhone:
The Start of a Mobile Health Revolution

Sebastien Tanguay, Vice President, Sales and Marketing, Myca
Peter Heywood, Principal, Industry Brand Agency

The Vision

We all know that the U.S. healthcare system is under increasing strain, and there is growing consensus that radical surgery is required. Doctors face extraordinary pressures to provide effective care while dealing with overflowing waiting rooms, keeping up with ever-changing information on procedures and medications and dealing with patients who are increasingly well informed, thanks to the internet. Healthcare consumers face a consultation and care process that seems remote, uncaring and optimized for everyone's needs but their own. They are increasingly being asked to manage their own health care expenses, and they need and want expert guidance to help them through the vast amounts of information available on the web.

We are convinced that mobile technology will play a central role in the reinvention of healthcare to address these challenges. We envision a healthcare system that leverages the full potential of mobile to improve the quality, effectiveness—and humanity—of care.

Mobile phones with video capability provide a new means of engagement that is cost effective and convenient yet virtually as personal as a face-to-face visit with a doctor. To date, however, the medical sector has been very slow in adopting this personal and portable means of communicating. Our mission is to provide the tools and create the demand to help change the sector's reluctance. Our first initiative is MyFoodPhone, a mobile-based nutrition information and tracking service.

MyFoodPhone: Shoot—Send—Get Feedback

To develop an understanding of this new market we were entering, we decided to develop a product that would link healthcare experts to consumers, in a sector of the market that is a manageable size. We chose the nutrition and diet sector, and launched MyFoodPhone, the world's first nutrition service linking individuals with their personal dietitian using a mobile device.

Some of the biggest challenges for those trying to change their eating habits are knowing what they are doing right and where they may need to improve, and staying motivated along the way. The goal of MyFoodPhone is to give dieters a fun, easy and more convenient way to keep a food journal and provide nutrition information that is specifically tailored for them.

MyFoodPhone is based on the use of camera phone images and video feedback. The unique mobile food-journaling application of this service helps customers monitor what they eat and helps them modify their eating habits. Furthermore, it helps them to achieve their individual health goals through motivation provided by personalized counseling from MyFoodPhone dietitians.

How it Works

MyFoodPhone is designed to be simple and intuitive—a tool that users can easily integrate into their everyday lives. The application involves three steps:

Step 1: Take a snapshot of all the food you eat.

Before eating or drinking anything, the user takes a snapshot of the food with his or her mobile phone.

Step 2: Send the photos to your food journal.

After taking the picture, the user simply sends it to an e-mail address. The picture is then stored in a personal food journal. The food journal is a log where pictures are stored by days of the week and type of meal (breakfast,

lunch, dinner, snack). The user can log into this food journal and add information to each picture. As we like to say, a picture is worth a thousand calories!

Step 3: Get feedback from your dietitian.

On a regular basis, depending on the individual user's plan, a MyFoodPhone dietitian provides personalized feedback and coaching in the form of a video message, helping users to stay motivated and increasing the likelihood that they

will achieve their goals. The analysis and tips are based on information and goals provided by the user at the outset of the program.

Building a Community of Users

Group support has proven to have positive benefits when it comes to helping people modify their lifestyle habits, as demonstrated by Alcoholics Anonymous® and Weight Watchers®. With that in mind and with the growth of web-

based social communities, we have created the MyFoodPhone Community as a complement to the basic application. The MFP Community is a tool and destination where friends, family and all people with a common goal or similar interests can share information, and more importantly, support each other in a fun and efficient way.

The MFP Community enables its members to

- share their food journals with their MyFoodPhone buddies to get helpful tips and motivating feedback

- share ideas about cooking, vegetarian eating, managing diabetes, how to avoid that candy bar and more

- find friends for one-on-one support or buddies with similar interests

The MFP Community members benefit from the power of a group to help them in their quest for better nutrition, and to meet their challenge of sticking to their nutritional plans and achieving their goals. As the community evolves, the obvious extension of the community onto the mobile platform, through SMS, voice and video calls, will provide significant added value.

What We Have Learned

After two years of operating the MyFoodPhone service, we have learned some valuable lessons that we will leverage in our future ventures. Based on our experience to date, we have learned five lessons about what it takes to develop a successful mobile health application:

Lesson 1: Taking and sharing pictures improves behavior.

Taking a picture of one's food and sending it to a journal is easy to do but has an important effect on users and their food consumption. It forces users to think, "Am I really hungry?" or "Do I really need to eat this chocolate bar?" and provides compulsive eaters enough time to change their minds about when, and what, they eat. In addition, knowing that others will know what they ate motivates users to make more sensible food choices.

Lesson 2: Personalized feedback is motivating.

There are thousands of books, magazines and websites devoted to diet and nutrition, but none of them is tailored for a single individual. What motivates MyFoodPhone customers is that every message, every tip every piece of information is specifically chosen for them by a credible source, based on their individual needs and goals. Moreover, the dietitian can illustrate the information with concrete examples in the users' food journal, further personalizing the experience.

Lesson 3: Video interaction has the same high impact as face-to-face meetings.

The human element in the MyFoodPhone experience has been key. Our experience has affirmed our initial assumption that the strength of the relationship between the user and the dietitian would directly correlate with successful outcomes. This is why, when creating the application, we thought it was essential to ensure that feedback from the MyFoodPhone dietitian was done in video format, as opposed to messaging or voice. Video was the closest we could get to the impact of a face-to-face meeting without losing the convenience and cost-effectiveness of a mobile application.

Lesson 4: Making it fun keeps it engaging.

Being on a diet or simply improving nutrition habits requires both desire and discipline. How many people do you know who have stayed on a diet for more that two months? We believed that if we were to succeed in persuading people to change their eating habits over time, the experience would have to be fun and easy. That's why we chose to go the "picture" route. We have seen with our subscribers that picture taking becomes second nature, removing a barrier to sustaining the effort to adopt better eating habits.

Lesson 5: Convenience = Compliance = Success

The convenience of mobile and the ease of access to expertise reinforce positive behavioral changes that lead to success, in our experience. It is clear that in order to succeed, a mobile service must be integrated with the user's behavior patterns. We achieved this by

- not requiring users to carry a separate device (we all carry our mobile phones with us)

- allowing users to maintain their schedules (the MyFoodPhone experience is asynchronous)

- not forcing users to learn a new technology (all they need to know is how to take a picture with their mobile phones)

The Next Step: A Doctor in Your Pocket

The future of our MyFoodPhone platform will be a series of applications that connect healthcare professionals with consumers and patients.

The next application that we plan to launch in the primary healthcare market is BabyPhone, a device and suite of services aimed at expectant and new mothers and their obstetricians and pediatricians. Consumers in this segment of the healthcare market are motivated by concerns over neonatal or child health issues; are younger and thus more accustomed to mobile and PC technology; are interested in information, services and products associated with health, wellness and nutrition for themselves and their children; and want to share information, images and videos with family and friends.

While the personal computer is a vital tool in helping consumers and doctors manage the complexities of healthcare, the new generation of video-enabled wireless devices creates opportunities to change how healthcare is delivered. MyFoodPhone has shown that people are willing to use mobile devices to manage health-related issues, and that it is an efficient way to deliver the counsel that helps them attain healthier lifestyles. The combination of greater health awareness, an aging Baby Boomer population, limited in-person access to healthcare professionals and the pervasiveness of rich-media mobile all indicate that our approach will become a part of people's lives, and an essential component of healthcare delivery in the future.

About the Authors

Sebastien Tanguay, who holds a B.A.A. in marketing from Laval University, has been leading MyFoodPhone Nutrition Inc., a mobile-health application service provider, since its foundation four years ago. He has played a major role in getting the company to sign an exclusive distribution agreement with a major U.S. cell phone carrier and has brought the company to its current state. Prior to joining MyFoodPhone, Sebastien was a brand manager for a 25-million-user software company called Copernic. He managed the team that created branding and marketing strategies for powerful information—aggregating search products such as Copernic Agent, Copernic Shopper and Copernic Summarizer.

Peter Heywood is the marketing advisor for MyFoodPhone and principal of Industry Brand Agency, located in Toronto. Peter is a branding specialist who provides strategic brand, marketing, and customer engagement counsel to companies in today's fast-changing markets. Peter leads brand research and strategy activities and directs the work of the creative teams charged with bringing clients' brands to life across all touch points. He has worked in a variety of sectors, including information technology, financial services and retail, for companies in both Canada and the U.S.

Perspective 4

Persuasive Games on Mobile Devices

Ian Bogost, Founding Partner, Persuasive Games, LLC

> *How do videogames express ideas?* Without understanding how games can be expressive in a general sense, it is hard to understand how they might be persuasive.
>
> *How do videogames make arguments?* Videogames are different from oral, textual, visual, or filmic media. Thus, when they try to persuade, they do so in a different fashion from speech, writing, images, or moving images.
>
> *What are some design strategies for persuasive mobile games?* Such design approaches need to take into account both the unique persuasive properties of videogames and the unique properties of mobile technology.

This chapter explores the three questions highlighted above. By understanding how videogames persuade by expressing ideas and making arguments in specific ways, and by leveraging the unique properties of mobile technology, designers can create videogames with tremendous persuasion potential.

How Videogames Express Ideas

Videogames are good at representing the behavior of systems. When we create videogames, we start with some system in the world—traffic, football, whatever. Let's call this the "source system." To create the game, we build a model of that source system. Videogames are software, so we build the model by authoring code that *simulates* the behavior we want to focus on. Writing code is different from writing prose or taking photographs or shooting video; code models a set of potential outcomes, all of which conform to the same general rules. One name for this type of representation is *procedurality* (Murray 1997); procedurality is a name for computers' ability to execute rule-based behaviors. Videogames are a kind of procedural representation.

Consider some examples: *Madden Football* is a procedural model of the sport of American football. It models the physical mechanics of human movement, the strategy of different sets of plays, and even the performance properties of specific professional athletes. *Sim City* is a procedural model of urban dynamics. It models the social behavior of residents and workers, as well as the economy, crime rate, pollution level, and other environmental dynamics.

So, in a videogame we have a source system, and a procedural model of that source system. A player needs to interact with the model to make it work—videogames are interactive software; they require the player to provide input to make the procedural model work. When the player plays, he or she forms some idea about the modeled system, and about the source system it models. He or she forms these ideas based on the way the source system is simulated; that is to say, there might be many different ways of proceduralizing a system. One designer might build a football game about the strategy of coaching, while another might build one about the duties of a particular field position, such as a defensive lineman. Likewise, one designer might build a city simulator that focuses on public services and new urbanism (Duany, Plater-Zyberk, & Alminana 2003), while another might focus on Robert Moses-style suburban planning.

This is not just a speculative observation: it highlights the fact that the source system never really exists as such. One person's idea of football or a city or any other subject for a representation of any kind is always *subjective*.

The inherent subjectivity of videogames creates dissonance—gaps between the designer's procedural model of a source system and a player's subjectivity, preconceptions, and understanding of the simulation. This is where videogames become expressive: they encourage players to interrogate and reconcile their own models of the world with the models presented in

The inherent subjectivity of videogames creates dissonance—gaps between the designer's procedural model of a source system and a player's subjectivity, preconceptions, and understanding of the simulation. This is where videogames become expressive: they encourage players to interrogate and reconcile their own models of the world with the models presented in a game.

a game. While videogames are often considered playthings, this charge toward reconciliation can also make games challenging or disturbing. This "simulation gap" creates a condition of crisis in the player, which I've called "simulation fever" (Bogost 2006).

How Videogames Persuade

Most of the time, videogames create procedural models of fantasy lives, like that of the pro ballplayer *(Madden),* or a blood elf *(World of Warcraft),* or a space marine *(Doom).* But, we can also use this facility to invite the player to see the ordinary world in new or different ways. One way to use videogames in this fashion is for persuasion, to make arguments about the way the world works.

My approach to building and understanding "Persuasive Games" is different from B.J. Fogg's approach to "Persuasive Technology" (Fogg 2002). Instead of approaching the topic through the discipline of psychology, I approach it through the discipline of *rhetoric*. Rhetoric is a very old line of philosophical thought that focuses on the art of effective persuasion. It is a field that has its roots in classical oratory, but which Aristotle extended to philosophical deliberation as a means of considering arguments.

I suggest combining rhetoric with the procedural representation we get in games, described above. The result would be a particular kind of rhetoric, one focused on the art of using processes persuasively, just as oral rhetoric focuses on using the spoken word persuasively, and visual rhetoric on using images persuasively. I call this new form of rhetoric "procedural rhetoric" (Bogost 2007).

> Since procedural models are inherently subjective, designers can make models of how they *think* things work or *don't* work, or how they *wish* they worked. Such models need not represent aspects of the material world, such as traffic or bridges. They can also represent what is abstract or conceptual, such as social practices, public policy, and everyday experiences.

Since videogames are procedural models of things in the world, procedural rhetoric is particularly useful for making claims about how things work by making models of how they work, rather than just describing their function through words or images. Furthermore, since procedural models are inherently subjective, we can also make models about how we *think* things work, or how they *don't* work, or how we *wish* they worked. The models we build need not represent just material things like traffic or bridges either—they can also represent abstract and conceptual things like social practices, public policy, and everyday experiences. Persuasive Games, then, are videogames that mount effective procedural rhetorics.

Persuasive Design for Mobile Games

Persuasive Games is not only the name I give to games of this kind. It is also the design philosophy that my commercial game studio uses to create games about topics such as global petroleum, agribusiness, disaffected copy store workers, and nutrition. However, designing such games for mobile devices requires not only an understanding of procedural rhetoric but an appreciation for the unique affordances of mobile devices.

When designing mobile persuasive games, one could treat mobile devices as just another microcomputer, applying the representational strategies I've described above to the smaller form factor of the mobile phone. But such an approach doesn't take into consideration the social or "mobile" aspects of such devices.

Likewise, one might target specific demographics that use mobile devices. For example, teenagers might be a desirable target for a particular social message, or perhaps executives with handheld PDA devices. But this too doesn't take into account the unique properties of mobile devices, just some of the kinds of people who use them.

One notable property of mobile devices is our ability to use them fluidly out in the world. The values we associate with this kind of mobility often have to do with the ubiquity of access and control; values such as seamlessness, immediacy, and transparency pervade such notions. This is a ubicomp-influenced dream of a frictionless networked world of total and complete presence—a Bloomberg terminal for everything.

But if we recall the gap between the procedural representation in a videogame and the source system that the game models, we might fall upon another approach: using mobile devices' properties of presence and location to *amplify difference and incongruity* rather than to remove them. This technique recalls the artistic technique of *defamiliarization*, which compels the viewer to see the ordinary in a new and unfamiliar way.

Airport Insecurity

As an example of this kind of mobile persuasive game design, consider a game we created at Persuasive Games. *Airport Insecurity* (Persuasive Games 2005) is a mobile game about the Transportation Security Administration (TSA). In the game, the player takes the role of a passenger at any of the 138 most trafficked airports in the USA. The gameplay is simple: The player must progress through the security line in an orderly and dignified fashion, taking care not to lag behind when space opens in front of him, as well as to avoid direct contact with other passengers (Figure 1a).

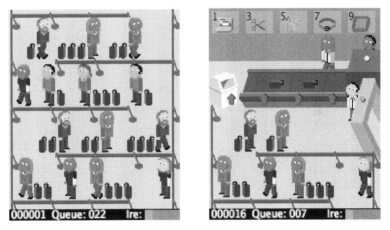

Figure 1 *Screens from* Airport Insecurity. *a) waiting in line in the game;*
b) reaching the front of the security line with items randomly assigned by the game.

When he reaches the x-ray check, the player must place his luggage and personal items on the belt. The game randomly assigns luggage and personal items to the player, including "questionable" items such as lighters and scissors, as well as legitimately dangerous items like knives and guns (Figure 1b).

For each airport, we gathered traffic and wait-time data to model the flow of the queues, and we also gathered as much as we could find in the public record on TSA performance. General Accountability Office (GAO) analysis of TSA performance used to be reported publicly, but the agency reportedly started classifying the information after it became clear that it might pose a national security risk. The upshot of such tactics is that the average citizen has no concept of what level of security they receive in exchange for the rights they forego. While the U.S. government wants its citizens to believe that increased protection and reduced rights are necessary to protect us from terrorism, the effectiveness of airport security practices is ultimately uncertain. The game made claims about this uncertainty by modeling it procedurally: players get to choose if they will dispose of their dangerous items in a trash can near the x-ray belt, or test the limits of the screening process by carrying them through.

Nothing I've mentioned so far about *Airport Insecurity* couldn't have been done on a non-mobile platform. But we chose the mobile phone as the platform for this game precisely because we wanted players to *play the game while in line at airport security*. When in queue at airport security, many of us file blindly through without asking ourselves how well or justly security actually operates. By inviting the player to explore a videogame-based model of the very experience they were taking part in, we hoped to amplify their estrangement by collapsing the source system and the procedural system on top of one another. No platform other than mobile would have made this possible.

> We chose the mobile phone as the platform for our *Airport Insecurity* game precisely because we wanted players to play the game *while in line at airport security*. By inviting the player to explore a videogame-based model of the very experience they were taking part in, we hoped to amplify their estrangement by collapsing the source system and the procedural system on top of one another. No platform other than mobile would have made this possible.

Cruel 2 B Kind

Consider another example, this one a live action game played via text messaging on mobile phones in a real-world environment. *Cruel 2 B Kind,* which ubiquitous game researcher and designer Jane McGonigal and I created, is a modification of games like *Assassin* in which players attempt to surreptitiously eliminate each other with predetermined "weapons" such as water pistols. But in *Cruel 2 B Kind*, players "kill with kindness"—each player is assigned a "weapon" and "weakness" that corresponds with a common, even ordinary pleasantry. For example, players might compliment someone's shoes, or serenade them.

While *Assassin* is usually played in closed environments such as college dorms, *Cruel 2 B Kind* is played in public, on the streets of New York City or San Francisco or anywhere in the world. Players not only don't know who their target is, they also don't know who is playing! In these situations, players are forced to use guesswork or deduction to figure out whom they might target. As a result, players often "attack" the wrong groups of people, or people who are not playing at all. The reactions to such encounters are startling for all concerned; after all, exchanging anonymous pleasantries is not something commonly done on the streets of New York (Figure 2).

Figure 2
Cruel 2 B Kind
participants on
the streets of
New York City.

Cruel 2 B Kind asks the player to layer an alternative set of social practices atop the world they normally occupy. Instead of ignoring their fellow citizens, the game demands that players interact with them. This juxtaposition of game rules and social rules draws attention to the way people do (or more properly, don't) interact with one another in everyday life. Mobile devices orchestrate this experience by delivering weapons of kindness and allowing players to record and track their score.

Airport Insecurity and *Cruel 2 B Kind* both focus on social and political practices—the way people interact with their government and with each other. But we can also imagine using defamiliarization as a mobile design strategy in the service of more traditional areas of influence.

For example, consider a hypothetical mobile phone game about health and nutrition. The game would be designed to intervene in everyday situations such as dining out or shopping for groceries, where consumers are more likely to make poor nutritional decisions. B.J. Fogg (2002) has previously discussed the notion of timeliness as a technique for persuasive technology, and certainly timeliness would be part of a nutritional intervention. But adding defamiliarization might accentuate the player's understanding of the gap between good and bad nutritional decisions.

For example, imagine that the mobile game allowed the player to choose a level that corresponded with the type of food the player was about to eat (e.g., fast food hamburger, or grocery store frozen meal). The game might offer the player a level or scenario based on a regular diet of that food stuff. How easy or difficult might it be to climb stairs, run a race, or play with one's grandchild after fifty years of eating burgers?

Disruptive and Strange

As players, we come to a videogame with an idea of the world and how it works. A game presents a model of that same world, but that model has its own properties that likely differ from our own. When we put the two models together, we see where they converge and diverge—this is what we do when we play games critically. One of the promising and largely unexplored features of mobile devices is their ability to collapse a representation and the situation it represents onto one another, making the convergences and dissonances more apparent. Mobile devices thus offer a particular opportunity to present procedural arguments that produce player deliberation—not by making those arguments seamless and comfortable, but rather by making them disruptive and strange.

> Mobile devices offer the opportunity to present procedural arguments that require players to deliberate—not by making those arguments seamless and comfortable, but rather by making them disruptive and strange.

Mobile persuasive games offer a particularly promising tool for intervention precisely because videogames are so adept at creating fictional worlds. That is to say, mobile persuasion has power not only because mobile devices can easily insert aspects of the real world into daily life, but also because they can insert aspects of imaginary worlds into daily life.

About the Author

Ian Bogost is a videogame designer and researcher. He is assistant professor at the Georgia Institute of Technology, and founding partner at Persuasive Games LLC (persuasivegames.com). He is author of Unit Operations: An Approach to Videogame Criticism (the MIT Press 2006) and of Persuasive Games: The Expressive Power of Videogames (the MIT Press 2007), and numerous articles on videogame culture and criticism. His videogames about topics as varied as airport security, disaffected employees, the petroleum industry, and tort reform have been played by millions of people and exhibited internationally. He is currently working on a book about the Atari 2600, and a game about the politics of nutrition.

Citations

Bogost, I. (2006). Unit Operations: An Approach to Videogame Criticism. Cambridge, MA: the MIT Press.

Bogost, I. (2007). Persuasive Games: The Expressive Power of Videogames. Cambridge, MA: the MIT Press◗

Duany, A., Plater-Zyberk, E., & Alminana, R. (2003). The New Civic Art: Elements of Town Planning. New York: Rizzoli Publications.

Fogg. B. (2002). Persuasive Technology: Using Comptuers to Change What We Think and Do. San Francisco: Morgan Kauffman.

McGonigal, J. & Bogost, I. (2006). Cruel 2 B Kind. http://www.cruelgame.com.

Murray, J. (1997). Hamlet on the Holodeck: The Future of Narrative in Cyberspace. New York: Free Press.

Persuasive Games (2005). Airport Insecurity. Atlanta: Persuasive Games. http://www.persuasivegames.com/games/game.aspx?game=airportinsecurity.

Perspective 5

Simply Persuasive: Using Mobile Technology to Boost Physical Activity

Erik Damen, CEO, Pam bv

Although the majority of people seem to know that moving your body is good for you, a discouragingly small proportion of people are doing it. Our modern society makes it very easy for us not to be active at all, but one of the main reasons is that we just don't know how much we should be moving, how much we are actually moving, and we lack the motivation to get moving.

When I was confronted with the rather bulky and user-unfriendly accelerometer technology in 1996 via the University of Maastricht in The Netherlands, I was also thinking a lot about service applications on the Internet. As a physicist, I was already interested in moving bodies, but I realized that moving human bodies could be even more fascinating. I saw an opportunity for a sleek consumer version of a scientific device based on accelerometers, as opposed to the already available cheap pedometers, in combination with an online personal coach, as a solution for people who want to become more physically active but need to be motivated to get moving.

The Personal Activity Monitor (Pam)

In 2000 I started a business to develop the technology—a simple device I called Pam, for Personal Activity Monitor. Personal activity monitors can show people how active they actually are (which is often less active than they think) and increase their understanding and consciousness about their physical activity. Our goal in developing Pam was to show how engaging, motivating and fun a personal activity monitor combined with an online, interactive coach, can be. We believed that if we could motivate people to become more active, we could have an impact on their health and quality of life.

Figure 1 The Personal Activity Monitor (Pam), designed to be simple to use and to provide an accurate estimation of daily energy expenditure. Unlike similar devices such as step counters, users are not required to input personal data, such as weight and height. Just take it out of the box and clip it on.

Pam was one of the first mobile persuasive technologies on the market. Now, almost seven years later, we have learned a lot. We have improved the technology so that its accuracy is very close to what can be measured by expensive exhaled gas analyzers. Pam is also far better than an ordinary pedometer, which counts steps only and can't differentiate between walking and running.

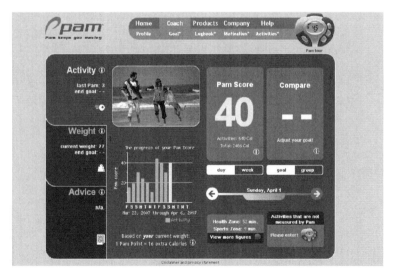

Figure 2 The Pam website shows users their personalized results and provides advice on how to achieve their goals.

How Pam Motivates Users

Pam monitors energy expenditure throughout the day and reports it in a way that is motivating to the user. Pam uses accelerometers to measure energy expenditure. There appears to be a direct relationship between acceleration of the body and the metabolic equivalent (MET)—a common measure of energy expenditure.[1] Pam expresses the user's activity as a derivative of the MET. Because the MET average over a day would be not much more than 1—a number we considered too small to be very motivating—we introduced a new metric called the Pam Score, which is equal to the MET score minus 1 times 100.

One attractive feature of the Pam Score is that, unlike calories, it is weight independent. As a result, the Pam Score enables people with very different body types to compare their physical activity, and thus has the potential to be more motivating than counting calories.

Another motivational aspect of Pam is the online coaching site that is a part of the product offering. Pam can be connected to a computer via a USB cable, and the memory read and uploaded automatically to the Pam coaching site. At the site, users are directed to their own personal space where they not only can find their physical activity data but can communicate with friends, be part of a group, play games, and share pictures. The unique combination of a measuring device and a coaching website creates the motivation to generate behavioral change.

Motivating and Facilitating Behavioral Change with Technology

In the course of our research, we identified seven important ingredients of a successful mobile persuasive technology, all of which we incorporated into Pam:

Biofeedback. If you want to effect change, measure what you want to change and make the information personal. Measuring personal activity is the first step, just like measuring body weight is the first step in weight loss.

Automatic data input. Collected measurement data should be fed into a database automatically, without the need for human intervention. People like convenience.

Motivating and Facilitating Behavioral Change (continued)

Goals. Goals stretch us, push us, and enable us to do things that we would otherwise avoid doing, or doing as well. An online personal coach helps people to set realistic goals.

Rewards. People like payoffs for their efforts. Rewards can be virtual trophies, new skins for their personal space on the site, and discount vouchers for an online shop.

Community. Community web-based portals have soared in popularity. Whatever behavior is desired, if it's shared with a group then the likelihood of adopting and maintaining the behavior increases. Connect a personal activity monitor to a web-based community of users and suddenly you are not just reading your personal stats, but chatting with another user and sharing a common experience, all of which increases motivation.

Games. Gaming engages people and increases personal performance. Gaming also creates identity and promotes social contribution. Pam leverages the power of gaming to motivate users. The total daily Pam scores of different groups can be compared each day. When the difference exceeds a certain preset value, one group has won the game. We have found that this very simple game has a motivating effect on users.

Identity. The success of MySpace surprised most people. Who would have thought you could get 80 million people to go to a web portal for no apparent reason other than to have their own space? People want identity. Web portals that incorporate this element into their design strategies strike a fundamental chord of human values.

Encouraging Results

In the last two years, we have attracted many members to our website, which is based on the personal coach model and features goal setting, advice, and results feedback (the community and game features were not yet installed on the site). When members used the existing Pam device and basic website for at least three months, the vast majority (69%) became more active, as shown in Figure 3.

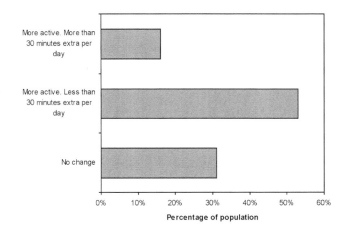

Figure 3 Change in activity of Pam website users. After three months, 69% of the population increased their activity level. Within that group, 16% increased their level of moderate activity by more than 30 minutes per day.

The fact that about 16% of Pam users increased their activity by more than the U.S. Surgeon General recommends (half an hour of moderate activity each day), shows that Pam's methodology has a strong ability to induce positive behavior change in many users.

Future Directions

Although we have shown that using our Personal Activity Monitor and website that provides feedback on how well users are doing can have a dramatic effect on behavior, we believe we can do better. We believe that an improvement of the web experience would increase the "stickiness" of the site and thus would prolong the results achieved. The longer people maintain a certain behavior, such as increasing their level of physical activity, the greater the chance that they will maintain the desired lifestyle.

Recently a new, Flash website based on community and gaming, but including the personal coaching features of the old Pam website, was launched (Figure 4). We expect the new site to have a higher level of stickiness. Further, we are considering combining the online service with mobile phone services, such as simple text messages that remind users to connect to the site again. When mobile phones become more advanced and mobile internet becomes more common, the next step would be to connect

Pam to your mobile phone via a wireless interface, allowing for even more immediate feedback and online fun.

Figure 4
The new Pam website allows users to convey their identities, participate in games, and share their achievements with friends.

Mobile persuasion is about more than applications on mobile phones. Wearing a device every day that measures your level of physical activity and combines it with an engaging, motivating website that helps you keep up the good work, is another compelling example of mobile persuasive technology.

End Notes

[1] MET is calculated as the ratio of total energy consumption to the basal metabolic rate.

About the Author

Erik Damen is the founder of Pam bv. He has a Ph.D. in physics. At Philips Electronics he worked in research, development, and marketing. Erik's long-term goal is to stimulate many users in many countries to follow through on their best intentions of self improvement and to become more physically active.

Citations

Eyre, H, Kahn, R, Robertson, RM, et al. "Preventing Cancer, Cardiovascular Disease, and Diabetes: A Common Agenda for the American Cancer Society, the American Diabetes Association, and the American Heart Association", Circulation 109(25), 3244–3255 (2004).

Blair, SN, LaMonte, MJ and Nichaman, MZ, "The evolution of physical activity recommendations: how much is enough?", Am J Clin Nutr 79(suppl), 913S–920S (2004).

Perspective 6

Managing Chronic Disease through Mobile Persuasion

Peter Boland, Business Development Director, BeWell Mobile Technology, Inc.

Over half of healthcare spending in the United States is attributed to just six chronic conditions: asthma, coronary artery disease, congestive heart failure, chronic obstructive pulmonary disease, depression, and diabetes. In contrast to acute illness, with proper self management, many chronic disease complications are avoidable. Self-management is critical because the day-to-day responsibility for monitoring and managing a chronic illness is borne largely by the patient. Care for chronic disease does not occur in a hospital or medical office setting. It occurs at home or at work—wherever the patient is, 24/7.

One of the most practical ways to use technology to intervene in chronic diseases and to bring needed behavioral change is through mobile phones rather than personal computers. While patients readily turn to PCs to look up information on the internet, they do not use them to actively monitor and manage their care every day. Unlike desktop computers and stationary monitoring devices, mobile phones are ubiquitous and portable. They offer immediacy and convenience.

In order for healthcare interventions to be successful, however, mobile phone applications must be designed for each of these unique diseases in order to support patients in self-management behaviors.

Case Example: Asthma Management

BeWell Mobile developed an asthma management application for children and teens with severe and persistent asthma in San Mateo County, a large urban county south of San Francisco. Patients were low-income earners, primarily Spanish speaking, and "frequent flyers" at the San Mateo Medical Center. The objective was to reduce unnecessary emergency room use for asthma-related conditions by training patients and their families in how to self-manage asthma.

In conjunction with the hospital's medical team, BeWell Mobile designed an easy-to-use application for monitoring symptoms and collecting relevant medical information. The application asks specific questions about symptoms. The patient clicks through to the correct answer rather than keying in individual letters or words.

Patient-generated information is transmitted to the server and web portal, which initiates an automatic response based on predefined clinical parameters set by the clinical team. Medical algorithms built into the application educate patients about what symptoms to monitor and track (e.g., night coughing, wheezing, tightness in the chest, reduced exercise, stress level) and what action to take (e.g., change medication amount or frequency, contact the physician).

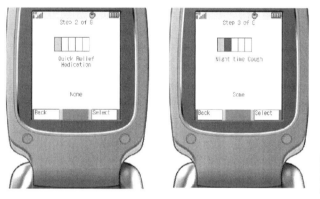

Figure 1
Medical intake and symptoms.

The application graphically indicates trends and takes patients through their daily action plans step by step. Patients "learn by doing" each day. Likewise, patients know they are being monitored, and this influences compliance.

Patients with asthma have more than enough reason to change behaviors and comply with an agreed-upon medical regimen: it will help them better manage their condition. Nevertheless, three important elements for success are often lacking: specific planning, stage-specific coaxing, and creating a sense of self-efficacy—step by step. Self-efficacy is key to building and maintaining the motivation to stay with a program; it involves a combination of beliefs and skills. Patients must develop the requisite skills to manage their condition and believe that these new skills are paying off.

Once they decide to change their behavior, patients require support to maintain healthy behaviors and avoid relapse. The latter results in a sense of failure and loss of self confidence.

BeWell Mobile applications are designed to support patients at each stage of their condition and at different motivational levels. This is done by identifying medically relevant choices and actions that can be taken at all times—when they get started, as they continue through their daily regimen, and if they relapse and need to start over again. Feedback is immediate (to counter inertia) and supportive (to build self confidence).

Each persuasive technique in the application is combined with positive feedback and encouragement. Personalized messages are a key component for increasing adherence and buy-in (Figure 2).

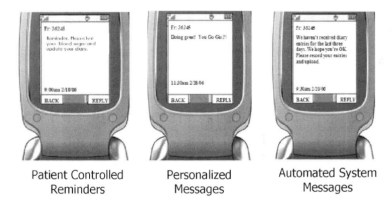

| Patient Controlled Reminders | Personalized Messages | Automated System Messages |

Figure 2 Personalized and automated messages.

Case Example: Diabetes Management

Education is one of the building blocks of changing behavior and is critical for managing diabetes. Because diabetes is a complex disease with many side effects, mobile phone applications help patients consider the advantages and disadvantages of making changes, show them what to do about their condition with step-by-step feedback, and encourage them to keep on course through repeated motivational messages. Relevant medical feedback and tailored messages reinforce the patient's intentions to change behavior. The communication is immediate and it is directly linked to their performance.

BeWell Mobile developed a diabetes management application for adult patients of a large health plan in southern California. One of the most important objectives was to build in flexibility so that patients could set reasonable goals and clinical teams could focus on different factors and conditions that drive diabetes (e.g., insulin usage, eating habits, blood pressure, depression, weight, level of activity, and stress level) as well as comorbidities commonly associated with the disease, such as hypertension and depression.

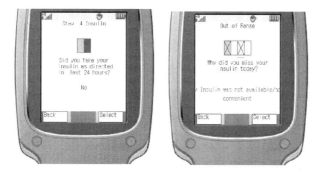

Figure 3
Insulin intake
questions.

As persuasive techniques, application features are used to engage patients with diabetes in five ways:

- Data collection by the patient

- Monitoring by the medical team

- Feedback based on medical algorithms

- Stage-specific health education

- Repeated motivational messages

At different times in the behavior change process, BeWell Mobile software applications play the role of teacher, coach, and self-management coordinator. Interactive software applications are designed to give patients many choices about *what* (content), *when* (frequency), and *how* (format) to interact with providers. This creates buy-in and engages the patient. By asking patients to respond to simple questions about their symptoms and conditions (by clicking on the right answer), they become more familiar with what medical triggers to look for and this increases their knowledge about how to manage their condition. They gain self confidence in the process and, through repetition, develop new habits and adopt healthier behaviors as a result.

Figure 4
Hypertension
monitoring
and
feedback.

BeWell Mobile Experience

As shown by patients trying to manage asthma and diabetes, chronic care patients need four essential ingredients to successfully manage their condition:

- Motivation
- Know-how
- Easy-to-use tools
- Self confidence

These requirements go hand in hand; if any one element is missing, the process unravels. The solution lies in interactive software technology that encompasses each dimension simultaneously.

Chronic-care patients need four essential ingredients to successfully manage their condition: motivation, know-how, easy-to-use tools, and self-confidence. If any one element is missing, the process unravels.

By incorporating the four building blocks (i.e., motivation, know-how, easy-to-use tools, and self-confidence) into each application, BeWell Mobile's pilot projects in California demonstrated high levels of user satisfaction (95%) among patients and providers and a high level of adherence. In San

Mateo County, adherence in using a digital diary for same-day self monitoring was 72%, and 92% for second-day reporting. By using the mobile phone application in conjunction with case management, patients reduced their asthma-related emergency room utilization from an average of 3–5 visits a year to 0 (Boland 2006).

Key Learnings

Two of the most effective means for influencing patient behavior are to directly involve individuals in making decisions about their care, and to give them continuing feedback and support. However, based on BeWell Mobile's initial projects, the single most important application feature is ease of use. If the application is not easy to use, it simply will not be adopted. In order to increase acceptance of self-monitoring software applications, patients must be able to "get in and get out" in less than a minute. BeWell Mobile navigation tools are so simple and straightforward that patients find them largely intuitive.

In order for mobile phone applications to be widely adopted, they must not only be easy to use by patients but also make life easier and better for overworked medical teams. Providers need to be able to monitor and manage far greater numbers of patients without hiring additional staff to do so. Hospitals and medical offices are constrained by budget and the availability of trained personnel. The current

> If an application is not easy to use, it simply will not be adopted. In order to increase acceptance of self-monitoring software applications, patients must be able to "get in and get out" in less than a minute.

healthcare delivery system is simply not designed to handle the growing incidence and prevalence of chronic care conditions. One answer lies with patient engagement strategies, such as mobile phone applications.

Clinicians are now responsible for caring for more and more patients with fewer and fewer resources at their disposal. Different patient outreach techniques, such as lab reminders and medical appointment scheduling, can be efficiently done through mobile phone messaging as well.

Likewise, the BeWell Mobile system is designed to support the workload of clinicians by enabling them to efficiently monitor more patients and better focus their time and efforts. BeWell Mobile's reporting format (exception reports are downloaded onto the provider's computer screen) serves as a spreadsheet that gives case managers access to many patient records at a single glance. Patients are prioritized according to predetermined levels of risk and degree of compliance with the medical regimen. This frees the medical team from routinely spending too much time on patients that do not need personal attention, so that caregivers are able to give their time and attention to where it is needed most.

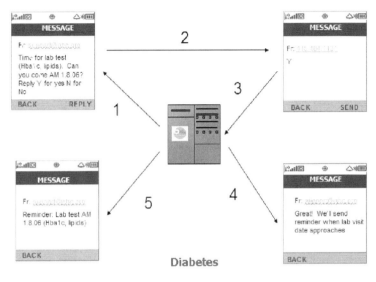

Figure 5 Diabetes lab reminders.

Conclusion

Mobile phones are well suited to support behavioral change for four reasons: the ubiquity and immediacy of handsets, their capacity to support behavior change, the availability of tailored software applications for different medical conditions, and the role of self management.

Regardless of location, people with chronic illness can compare how they are doing from one day to the next because mobile medical management applications automatically trend patient symptoms all week. If patient-reported symptoms indicate a decline in daily functioning, feedback is given immediately. This enables patients to adjust their behavior and medications in order to better manage their condition. The interplay between patients and their medical team, via the software application, increases self efficacy and improves self-management skills.

Moreover, mobile phones change behavior by creating a unique relationship between the patient and the device. Mobile handsets are far more than a telephone without a cord attached. They are like the fabled Swiss Army knife: a single multi-use practical tool. Because medical management applications reside on the handset, mobile phones become the patient's own "Asthma Assistant" or "Diabetes Assistant." As an interactive technology, mobile phones become an indispensable part of the individual's medical support system.

About the Author

Dr. Boland is a national thought–leader with 28 years of healthcare industry experience. He has been a management consultant to leading technology vendors, hospital systems, health plans, and purchasers. He has written numerous books on healthcare delivery (*Making Managed Healthcare Work* and *The New Healthcare Market*), clinical practice (*Physician Profiling and Risk Adjustment*), and management and market strategy (*Redesigning Healthcare Delivery* and *The Capitation Sourcebook*). He has also published in dozens of professional journals. He received a doctorate from UCLA, a masters degree from the University of Michigan, and a post-graduate certificate from Harvard University's Executive Program in Health Policy and Management.

Citations

Finkelstein, E.A., Fiebelkorn, I.C., Wang, G., "National medical spending attributable to overweight and obesity: How much, and who's paying? Health Affairs 2003; January-June; Supplement Web Exclusives: W3- 219–226.

Boland, P. (2007), "The Emerging Role of Cell Phone Technology in Ambulatory Care," Journal of Ambulatory Care Management, Vol.30, No.2, pp. 126–133.

Perspective 7

Augmented Reality:
Using Mobile Visualization to Persuade

Sean White, Ph.D. Candidate, Columbia University

Imagine yourself walking down a wooded path, when you notice a plant that you don't recognize. You're curious and want to know more about this botanical wonder: What is its name? How does it fit into the local ecosystem? Where did it come from? If you're lucky enough to be carrying a field guide or reference book on the local flora, you might slowly browse through the pages and find the plant, or you could take a photo and later ask a friend about the plant. In either case, you've removed your attention from the source of curiosity. Instead of simply knowing about the plant, you have to somehow identify it and then make an indirect association between the information on the page and the plant in the physical world. A similar scenario could be imagined in an urban setting.

In these examples, there is a gap between the environment and presentation of knowledge about the environment. What happens when we narrow the gap? How might this change our interaction with the world around us?

Figure 1a,b Visualization of virtual vouchers in tangible augmented reality.

At the Computer Graphics and User Interfaces lab at Columbia University, we are exploring this question through research into electronic field guides and mobile augmented reality (AR) systems (Figure 1a,b). This chapter discusses our research and its implications in more detail. Using mobile technology to augment real-world environments has powerful implications for persuasion, as our research is making clear.

Shifting the Locus of Interaction

Repositories of knowledge have historically been centralized in physical places like libraries, their books and manuscripts far distant from the topics on which they expound. In the 20th century, computation required people to gather around the computational artifact, whether it was a massive room full of tubes or a beige box on a desktop, to gain some benefit from the magic of computer processing. Like cavemen huddled around a fire, they were forced to a particular location centered on a precious resource. Over time, these resources have become portable and mobile. Books were mass-produced and safely carried out into the world. Computation and digital displays travel with us wherever we go in the form of mobile phones, PDAs and laptops.

Knowledge, computation, sensing and presentation have moved from monolithic and centralized to mobile and distributed. This shifts the locus of visualization and interaction into the environment and objects we encounter. Treated as extensions of perception and cognition, they change behaviors by changing how we view the world and our expectations about interacting with the environment. To explore this shift, we are investigating mobile user interfaces to an electronic field guide (EFG) for botanical species identification, visualization and collection.

Electronic Field Guides

Botanical Research

Biological research in the field, the test bed for our own research, is constrained by the speed and difficulty of species determination, as well as by access to relevant information about the species encountered. When botanists want to verify the identity of a plant species, they compare the sample plant with a voucher specimen found in repositories like the Smithsonian Institution Herbarium. During field research, this requires weeks or months of travel and transportation of fragile and unique plants. Species disappear faster than they can be identified for biodiversity studies.

> Mobile visualization, coupled with recent work on vision-based algorithms, raises the promise of rapid botanical species identification and provides opportunities for new user interface and visualization techniques.

However, mobile visualization coupled with recent work on vision-based algorithms raises the promise of rapid botanical species identification and provides opportunities for new user interface and visualization techniques. Columbia University, University of Maryland and the Smithsonian Institution are working together to develop an electronic field guide for botanists that supports vision-based automated species identification (Agarwal 2006).

Prototype Mobile Systems

The core electronic field guide changes the perception of plants in the environment by using computer vision to identify a plant species and mobile displays to immediately present results of the identification process visually to aid in collection of specimens. In addition, all contextual data about the sample and context, such as GPS location, collector and time/date, are stored in a database.

Hand held devices

To explore comparative forms of mobile visualization, we developed a 2D user interface, LeafView (Figure 2a), which uses a wireless digital camera to capture images of sample leaves and a tablet PC to segment, identify, visualize, collect, and interact with results of identification (White 2007). A zoomable user interface presents results and relevant information at a variety

Figure 2 (a) Visualization of matching leaf results.
(b) Species information augmenting the environment.

of semantic levels. Additional prototypes use a mobile phone, web page, or hand held ultra-mobile PC.

Tangible augmented reality

Our prototype 3D user interface (White 2006) uses a head-worn display and tangible augmented reality with vision-based tracking (Figure 1a) to overlay virtual search results, called virtual vouchers, onto the physical world associated with a sample leaf (Figure 1b). Virtual vouchers provide a holistic digital representation of an object in the physical world. In the case of plant species, the representation includes images at multiple scales, context, and characteristics of the plant, as well as specific collection information for samples of the species. This prototype supports physical interaction with virtual vouchers and manipulation of the visualization through 3D gestures and tangible interaction. For example, part of the prototype is a physical card that visually morphs into different virtual vouchers. The virtual representation can then be examined as if it were a physical plant, and morphed into different visual aspects of the species by spinning the card. An alternative visualization directly augments the environment (Figure 2b).

> Our prototype 3D user interface uses a head-worn display and tangible augmented reality with vision-based tracking to overlay virtual search results ("virtual vouchers") onto the physical world associated with a sample leaf.

Augmented Reality

Augmented reality refers to computer displays that add virtual information to a user's sensory perceptions (Feiner 2002). In doing this, AR systems overlay sensory information such as computer graphics or sound directly over the physical world. They require a display such as a head-worn or handheld display and a means of knowing where the physical world is in relation to the display. Instead of a blank 2D screen, the physical world becomes the canvas on which we paint. In this way, a virtual teapot can be placed on a physical table, virtual buildings can be placed on a city street, or a virtual plant can appear in a hand. There are numerous unsolved research problems in the field of augmented reality but early experiments show that we can situate visualizations in their spatial, physical world context.

Typically, visualizations are shown on a black background, stuck on a computer screen or perhaps inside a virtual reality display. In the figure–ground relationship, the ground or background has no meaning and no relationship to the visualization.

Meaning through the interaction of virtual and physical

Situated visualizations, on the other hand, gain meaning through the combination of the visualization and the relationship between the visualization and environment—for instance, seeing the movement of a botanical species visualized over time and overlaid on the physical hillside where the observer can see the way the physical world might have affected the transitions. New meaning emerges from the interaction between the virtual and real world. To some extent, all visualizations are situated, but I use the term here to specifically refer to visualizations that are presented in close spatial proximity to their relevant subject.

Association through proximity

An additional benefit then, is cognitive association through proximity. Seeing the name of a plant or related vouchers next to the leaf in the physical world brings the information in closer proximity than a list in a book. A book can change perceptions, but there is a temporal gap and a spatial gap between the observed and the augmentation. This creates a level of indirection in the association that must be filled by additional cognitive processes. In user interface design, it is the perceptual equivalent of comparing indirect control of an icon through text commands and direct manipulation of an icon with a finger.

> Seeing the name of a plant next to the leaf in the physical world brings the information in closer proximity than a list in a book.

Persuasive Augmentation

We now have the ability to interpret the world through computer vision and other sensors—for example, to identify a plant based on appearance. Our computational and knowledge resources are mobile and we can even augment the world by using it as a canvas. How then can we use these systems as persuasive technologies?

Shifting Behaviors in Existing Practices ...

Rather than replace old behaviors, LeafView takes advantage of existing behaviors. Mobility supports design intervention wherever the behavior may be. Our initial design was primarily focused on identification. While this was supported by the six botanists who are directly collaborating with us, some other botanists have reacted with some apprehension to the idea. We discovered these reactions at an exhibition of the LeafView prototype. Of the many botanists who used the system with our guidance at the exhibition, three (not our regular users) initially had hesitant reactions on hearing that this was a "plant identification system." However, they responded positively when they understood that it was a collection tool intended to assist rather than replace them in identification.

This difference in reaction appears to be due to the perception that a pure identification system is somehow replacing the botanist, while an intelligent collection system or electronic field guide maintains the locus of control with the botanist. While this may not be an issue for non-experts, it is worth remembering when designing for and presenting to groups with sensitivity toward their own knowledge. A relatively minor (to us) change in system emphasis made a significant difference in the perception—and adoption—of the system by potential users.

... and Encouraging New Behaviors

Biologists such as Maturana (Maturana & Varela 1980) suggest that changes to our environment change our biology and behaviors. Our form of engagement shapes our reality. If our augmentation affects the way we perceive the environment and our world, and we control the augmentation, then we can affect behaviors. If, for instance, we want to keep botanists from touching dangerous plants, we might surround such plants with a red halo, change their appearance or even hide them.

> Our form of engagement shapes our reality. If augmentation affects the way we perceive the environment and our world, and we control the augmentation, then we can affect behavior.

In our prototypes, the point is to speed decision and analysis in situ, in temporal and spatial proximity to plant samples. Where previously, such tasks might take months and distant travel away from the research site to identify plants, it now takes a few minutes and the attention of the botanist. It becomes natural behavior to make decisions and analysis in the field instead of waiting to return to the herbarium.

Changing Perception of and Attitudes Toward the Environment

Augmentation allows us to mediate perception in subtle ways. If we make it as simple and easy as looking at something to learn more about it, we encourage curiosity, learning, and understanding. We have a different relationship with things we can name and know. For example, we can draw attention to a particular plant, object, or place by simply highlighting it in our field of view. Preattentive cues and our perceptual hardware will kick in. There will always be mystery in the world around us, but by bringing attention to the environment, we encourage thinking about the environment. We also enable non-specialists to share in the experience of knowing about ecologies.

Designing a New Worldview

We started by bringing the herbarium to the environment but proceeded to find depth in the world around us. In our old worldview, a leaf was a leaf. But now the leaf, and any other object in the world, has something it can tell us.

Once we learn that our environment has more to say then we previously knew, we start to listen to it. It has even been suggested that we begin to coauthor and cocreate with our environment (Laurel 2006). If we are augmenting that environment, then coauthoring is mediated by the choices made in sensing the environment and during augmentation. Who decides what name is given to a plant? Who decides what gets sensed and how it is represented in our augmented reality? The notion of design and authoring becomes more complex here.

Looking Toward the Future

You won't see AR goggles with enhanced computer vision at the store any time soon, although you might see handheld AR displays popping up in the near future. The ability to augment the environment around us is exciting, but there's still much work to be done.

Although most of the examples here have focused on augmenting the botanical environment, we believe the concepts and techniques generalize to the world around us. While still easily distinguishable from physical reality, persuasive augmentation will eventually need to deal with big challenges like the subtleties of attention filtering in the physical world, representations of authorship, and the ethical implications of augmented, mediated, and shared points of view. Addressing these issues will further the positive impact of mobile visualization and persuasive augmentation, enabling us to know and coauthor our world in progressive ways.

About the Author

Sean White works in the areas of computer science, energy and the environment. As a Ph.D. candidate in computer science at Columbia University, his current project investigates mobile and augmented reality electronic field guides for botanical species identification, visualization and collection. His recent research in mechanical engineering included development of carbon nano-tubes for fuel cells and structuring of dye sensitized solar cells. His other projects include tangible visualization of urban environments, visual interfaces for mixed collaborative audio spaces, wearable personal audio recording, global web-based email and interactive installations at Lollapalooza.

Acknowledgements

This work was funded in part by National Science Foundation Grant IIS-03-25867. For more information about the project, visit http://herbarium.cs.columbia.edu and http://www.cs.columbia.edu/graphics/projects/efg.

This work is part of a large joint research project involving the efforts of Steven Feiner, Jason Kopylec, Dominic Marino, Peter Belhumeur, David Jacobs, John Kress, Ravi Ramamoorthi, Gaurav Agarwal, Haibin Ling, Nandan Dixit, Mark Korthals, Charles Macanka, Ida Lopez, Ellen Farr, Rusty Russell and Norm Bourg.

Citations

Agarwal, G., Belhumeur, P., Feiner, S., Jacobs, D., Kress, W.J., Ramamoorthi, R., Bourg, N., Dixit, N., Ling, H., Mahajan, D.,Russell, R., Shirdhonkar, S., Sunkavalli, K., and White, S. First steps toward an electronic field guide for plants. Taxon, Journal of the International Association for Plant Taxonomy, 55(3), Aug 2006, 597–610.

Feiner, S. (2002) "Augmented reality: A new way of seeing." Scientific American, April 24, 2002.

Laurel, B. (2006) Keynote for UbiComp 2006.

Maturana, H. , and Varela, F. (1980) Autopoiesis and Cognition: the realization of the living, Springer, 1980.

White, S., Feiner, S., Kopylec, J. (2006) Virtual Vouchers: Prototyping a mobile augmented reality user interface for botanical species identification. Proc. IEEE Symp. on 3D User Interfaces 2006, Alexandria, VA, March 25–26, 2006, 119–126.

White, S., Marino, D., Feiner, S., (2007) Designing a Mobile User Interface for Automated Species Identification, To appear in Proc. ACM CHI 2007, Apr 2007.

Transforming the Mobile Phone into a Personal Performance Coach

Alex Kass, Accenture Technology Labs

Imagine having a personal coach with you all the time, helping you target habits that matter to you. Depending on what your particular personal development goals are, you might picture this coach letting you know if you are interrupting colleagues too frequently, getting enough exercise, talking too much on a sales call, eating too much high-fat food, or managing your time effectively. Our group at Accenture Technology Labs has been developing a prototype software system called The Personal Performance Coach (PPC), which is designed to transform the mobile smartphone into such a coach–creating a device that can provide users with continuous, automated coaching on various behavior patterns they might be trying to form or to break.

Why Automated Coaching Matters— and How It's Becoming Feasible

Traditional training teaches learners the right thing to do, then hopes that they execute what they've learned correctly. But factors that shape our behavior go well beyond the up-front acquisition of knowledge that a training session can provide. As a result, even learners who show clear understanding of relevant principles and skills often fail to do the right thing when the moment of truth arrives. If, for instance, you are only dimly aware of your actual behavior patterns, you cannot hope to improve them, even if the general principles of effective behavior are clear to you. We believe that software such as our Personal Performance Coach will dramatically change the way we all understand and shape our own behaviors, providing us with both a deeper understanding of the behavior patterns that influence our personal and professional effectiveness and the discipline we sometimes need to make the day-to-day choices that align our behavior with our goals.

This new kind of automated coaching is made possible by two key technology trends: The first is the emergence of increasingly powerful pocket devices, which are currently called phones but are really powerful computers. For example, the leading edge smartphone currently on the market has a screen resolution that is the equal to that of my first laptop from a little more than a decade ago, and has comparable processing power and storage. What's more, it is capable of accessing network based resources via both Wi-Fi and cellular data transfer. The second trend involves the growing array of wearable wireless (Bluetooth) sensors that can be used in conjunction with these phones. By exploiting the fact that these mobile devices can always be with us, on our bodies, software such as our Personal Performance Coach can monitor many aspects of behavior, making possible a coach in your pocket that can provide near-real-time feedback on how well your actual behavior patterns match the goals you've set.

> Factors that shape our behavior go well beyond the acquisition of knowledge that a training session can provide. As a result, even learners who clearly understand relevant principles and skills often fail to do the right thing when the moment of truth arrives. If you are only dimly aware of your actual behavior patterns, you cannot hope to improve them, even if the general principles of effective behavior are clear to you.

How the Personal Performance Coach Works

It's important to note that the objective of our project was not to develop our own theories of how to conduct an effective meeting or sales call, or how to get in shape. That's the job of subject matter experts in each of those areas, of which many can be found on the shelves of the local bookstore. In other words, with this new coaching platform in place, a guru with an approach to, say, weight-loss, who might previously have been limited to writing a book or teaching a course, will be able to influence the behavior of those who buy into the theory through a PPC module, which would provide automatic coaching on the approach. Our own coaching theory is at the more abstract level–that these theories in general can be expressed in terms of observable behavior metrics, and that a standard set of interfaces can be developed to help learners see how their behavior compares with the targets they've chosen to pursue.

At least, that's the idea. To start realizing and testing that idea, we're creating our own demonstration modules based on simple approaches to shaping underlying behavior.

At a technological level, the Personal Performance Coach consists of software running on three different kinds of machines–the mobile phone, a server, and a laptop or desktop computer. Each does what it does best, and together they form a powerful distributed coaching system. Figure 1 illustrates the overall division of labor and communication pathways.

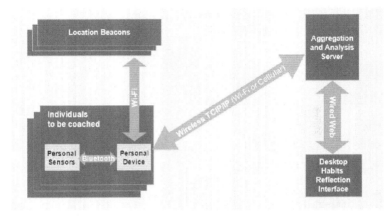

Figure 1 How elements of the Personal Performance Coach work together.

The mobile device collects data about the user's body and environment:
Our smartphone software buffers the data streams generated by wearable Bluetooth sensors, and transmits the data wirelessly to a server for analysis and long term storage.

The server analyzes these data streams and determines what coaching is needed: The server—not the phone—does the heavy lifting of integrating sensor streams from multiple devices, then analyzing the results to interpret the user's behavior and match it to the goals they have set. While some of the simpler analyses could probably be done on the phone, offloading the analysis to a server allows for more complex aggregation and computation, such as that required by the analysis of voice streams for conversation coaching. The server then transmits analysis and coaching instructions back to the mobile device in near-real-time, in the midst of the ongoing conversation.

The device provides immediate feedback: The smartphone can then deliver the coaching through various modalities—by whispering into the user's ear (via wireless headset), for instance, or through visuals that users may glance at even as they are engaged in the activity they are being coached on. Figure 2 illustrates some representative screenshots from the mobile device.

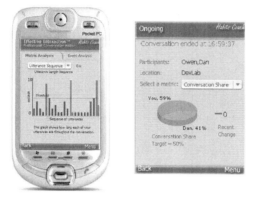

Figure 2
Examples of the Personal Performance Coach displaying metrics.

The PC provides more detailed feedback: A PC's larger screen provides the opportunity to provide more comprehensive views. This nicely complements the shallower, but more immediate feedback available on the mobile device. Figure 3 illustrates some representative displays from the desktop interface.

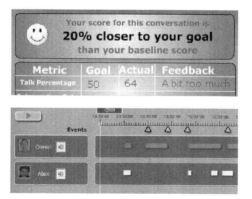

Figure 3
Detailed feedback provided on the desktop. (a) Feedback on progress for each metric. (b) Who was talking when, and how often did we talk over each other.

Of course, this approach is intended to be extensible to any behaviors that can be monitored with wearable wireless sensors. Sensors that we've currently been working with include the following:

- the microphone from a Bluetooth headset, for tracking users' speeches

- a GPS receiver, for tracking their movements outside (from building to building)

- the Wi-Fi signal detector, for tracking location within a building that's equipped with multiple Wi-Fi access points

- various biometric sensors, for tracking things such as heart rate and level of exercise

Example PPC Module: Tracking Conversation Habits

To illustrate how we imagine the Personal Performance Coach changing the way people shape their own behavior, let's briefly consider a usage scenario that we imagine might be typical: Imagine a busy professional, let's call him Joe. Joe works hard, but like most of us, he has some bad habits that sometimes affect both his job effectiveness and his personal well being. For example, one group of behavior patterns that can have significant impact in the workplace are related to group meetings. Let's imagine that in a recent performance review, Joe was told that this is an area in which he has significant room for improvement. In particular his staff and coworkers have complained that he is often late to meetings, often dominates the floor; fails to listen to what others have to say, interrupts, goes on for too long at a stretch without letting himself be interrupted and too frequently allows his meetings to go longer than planned.

If Joe is typical, he might be a bit defensive when he gets this feedback, and think it unfair; denial is one of the factors that keeps us from addressing our bad habits. This is where the PPC's module on conversation habits can help. To use it, Joe would install the PPC software on his smartphone, and would wear a wireless earpiece throughout the workday. (Note: Joe can get useful feedback on his behavior even if he is the only PPC user, though he and his colleagues can get even richer feedback if multiple members of the workgroup carry devices running the PPC software.)

The PPC system would then track Joe's meeting and conversation activity throughout the day. Using proximity detection technologies, the coach is capable of detecting when Joe is near coworkers who are also equipped with a smartphone, and can also detect which rooms throughout the building Joe enters. Using the headset, the system can tell when Joe (and his colleagues who are also equipped) is talking. The server software can use this location and voice information to identify and analyze Joe's meetings, based on the goals Joe has input into the system. For instance he could set a goal of talking no more than his fair share of the meeting time—say, 25%—or holding the floor for no more than two minutes at a stretch before stopping to allow colleagues to speak. The mobile device would then show, during each conversation, how his behavior metrics compare to his goals, and the desktop interface would allow Joe to see whether or not his behavior was getting closer to his goals over time.

Testing Our Assumptions

The PPC prototype we've developed makes an intriguing demo, but will this technology really prove useful? We can't know for sure until it is mature enough to pilot in daily use—the next key objective for our work. Development of the Personal Performance Coach is an ambitious project. Our technology concept is based on five assumptions, highlighted below. If these assumptions prove to be correct, we believe that the Personal Performance Coach could become a successful product.

Simple sensor signals can often serve as adequate proxies for detecting relevant behaviors. Research done at the MIT Media Lab on automated analysis of social signals (Pentland 2005) provides very suggestive evidence on this point. For instance, using very simple metrics, measured automatically, they could predict whether participants in a negotiation would view the negotiation as fair.

Merely making users aware of their actual behavior patterns, compared to their goals, will help them to improve. My own belief in this premise flows from my experience in weight loss programs, where the discipline of writing down what you eat plays a key role in rethinking and reforming problematic eating behaviors.

Occasional, gentle, real-time coaching will be welcome, not intrusive, once users acclimate. Evidence for this comes from the ease with which media professionals come to use ear prompters, after they've had a bit of time and practice getting used to them.

People will accept having a machine coach and critique them: It's quite difficult to know whether this will prove out or not, because it hasn't been possible on this scale before. However, acceptance of more traditional computer based training seems to suggest that it might, as long as the automated coach does not claim to know more than it actually does. In some ways, in fact, an automated coach might achieve more acceptance than a human one, since it is potentially less embarrassing than having another human review your habits.

Current hardware challenges will soon be overcome: The biggest current hardware limitation to making all this practical is probably the need to keep it powered continuously. But with advances such as low-power alternatives to Bluetooth emerging, it seems likely that this barrier will soon be overcome.

Conclusion

What is the potential of that powerful computer in your pocket? Of course, it will provide a new way to deliver content and services previously tied to the desktop. But we think that the Personal Performance Coach suggests that mobile phones could also enable something bigger, more radically new: The opportunity to help us reach a deeper level of awareness about our day to day behavior patterns. In the same way that we now take ubiquitous mobile telephony for granted, we may soon take for granted the availability of automated coaching that helps shape our behavior to make us more productive, healthier…and maybe even happier.

About the Author

Alex Kass is a senior researcher at Accenture Technology Labs, where he works to help the company anticipate technologies that will be important to the future of Accenture and its clients, and to invent prototypes that integrate these emerging technologies in new ways. Alex received his Ph.D. in computer science, with an emphasis on artificial intelligence, in 1990, and has spent his career working on issues at the intersection of computation and human cognition. His main focus is currently on various eLearning and performance support technologies, especially including intelligent workspaces, simulation-based training, next-generation business intelligence and mobile technologies for supporting improvements in personal effectiveness.

Citations

Pentland, Alex (2005). "Socially Aware Computation and Communication," *Computer*, March 2005, vol. 38, no. 3, pp. 33–40.

Perspective 9

Personal Health Assistant in the Palm of Your Hand

Paul Hedtke, Senior Director, Business Development, QUALCOMM, Inc.

The mobile phone has become an ideal platform for hosting highly personalized applications and delivering very "personal" services, such as those associated with health and wellness. I am currently working on a project that is intended to bring the concept of a mobile phone-based personal health assistant to fruition and more importantly, to market.

Working in concert with appropriate biometric sensor devices, the mobile phone automatically captures biological and physiological information as an individual navigates his or her typical day. In addition, the phone can be used to query the individual for relevant information input anywhere, anytime. This "personal health information" can be processed locally on the device, transferred immediately to a network-connected server for further processing and/or display for human analysis, and stored for later retrieval and analysis by a number of stakeholders, including the individual, his or her caregiver(s) and health providers. Conversely, the results of computer or human analysis of the personal health information can be conveyed immediately back to the user in the form of suggested actions, educational information, assessment of current health state, therapy reminders etc. The overall concept is depicted in Figure 1.

Making the interactions with the user compelling is the biggest challenge in developing health-related mobile applications. The mobile phone platform cannot simply be treated as a smaller version of the personal computer when it comes to interacting with the user. Conversely, the personal computer lacks the voice telephony capability inherent in the mobile phone platform. Both of these points need to be kept in perspective when implementing a mobile phone-based personal health assistant.

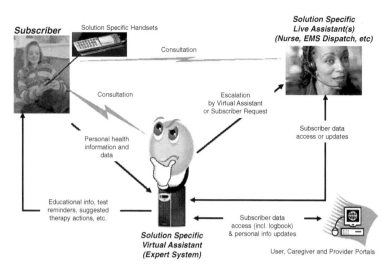

Figure 1 The mobile phone is an ideal platform for hosting highly personalized applications and delivering very "personal" services, such as those associated with health and wellness.

Collecting Personal Health Data

The concept of a "personal health assistant in your hand" who is always there, always vigilant, always relevant cannot be achieved without an effective means of monitoring the individual's health. If the data collection process is onerous or requires any more than minimal participation by the user, the concept will fail.

To the extent practical, collection of the biometric information needed to drive the personal health assistant must be accomplished without requiring any thought or action by the user. This means integrating biometric measuring devices into the mobile component of the solution. The mobile phone device itself can host certain types of measuring devices, but others must be worn on the body in order to achieve a continuous or semi-continuous collection of desired biometric information. To

If the data collection process is onerous or requires any more than minimal participation by the user, the concept will fail. To the extent practical, collection of the biometric information needed to drive the personal health assistant must be accomplished without requiring any thought or action by the user. This means integrating biometric measuring devices into the mobile component of the solution.

do this effectively and create a compelling solution that people will use requires direct collaboration with the biometric measurement products industry. "Velcro engineered" solutions generally are not compelling enough to achieve widespread adoption among the general public, as the typical consumer does not want the responsibility of system integration. The solution needs to work "out of the box," with all components fully functioning and interoperable.

Auto Profiling of the Individual

Another element of the personal health assistant is the creation of a user profile that the "assistant" function can reference as a baseline for determining the individual's health status, current "health affecting" behavior, and how the assistant can best provide assistance (which generally entails attempting to persuade users to change their behavior). It is unlikely that there will be an opportunity to fully profile the individual at the outset (i.e., upon service activation). A knowledge base (personal profile) can be built through successive interactions with the user, taking advantage of the fact that the phone is always with the individual and (almost) always "connected" via the wireless network.

Thus, the profiling process can be accomplished by a continuing series of queries—extracting information in bite size pieces so that the individual does not become annoyed or bored by a lengthy information capture process (as is typical of many "personal health assessments" associated with web-based solutions). Use of a "live profiler" can also be readily accommodated by the fact that the mobile phone is, after all, a voice communications device. While the phone platform is becoming a very capable handheld computer, and high speed network connectivity enables server assisted computing, human to human interactions are still a key element in any compelling personal health assistant implementation. Using a live profiler in the initial setup of a new user is an opportunity to also begin to create a "relationship" between the personal health assistant service and the new user.

The compelling implementation of a personal health assistant will integrate these virtual and human components into a unified, consistent entity that the user can come to depend upon, trust and accept without becoming disappointed, annoyed or bored.

The Virtual Assistant/Live Assistant Duality

The power of the mobile phone to deliver a personal health assistant into the palm of the hand of the individual lies in its extreme mobility, coupled with its ability to interact with the individual on a semi-continuous basis—both to monitor the individual's health state and to provide assistance to individuals in managing their health. Technology will enable the delivery of such services at a cost that is low enough to make the service affordable to the average individual.

> Technology can enable the delivery of personal health services at a cost that is low enough to make the service affordable to the average individual. However, an effective solution will also include a human element that can assist the virtual element as the need arises.

Thus, much of the "assistant" function can and should be implemented using technology (i.e., a "virtual," computer-generated, assistant is the primary "player"). However, an effective implementation will also include a human element that can assist the virtual element as the need arises.

Building an Effective Virtual Assistant

If the goal of any human interactive software is to persuade, inform, educate, enlighten or entertain, the user interface must be intuitive, easy to use, fun to use, dynamic, fresh and compelling. Creating an effective virtual health assistant that the user won't disable after the first couple of days requires creating a user experience that has all the attributes listed above.

High speed, low latency data communications between the phone device and network resident servers make it possible to continually change the method and media used to interact with the user, because the server can be readily updated with new content. Video, audio, text and graphics can all be utilized to deliver information to the user, or to query her or him for input when needing to extract information. Mixing and matching the different formats, and continually refreshing the content (by constant update on the server) makes it possible to deliver a compelling interaction that doesn't become repetitive or boring, and which creates a sense of "personalized" attention. In the case of a personal health assistant that is also heavily driven by personal health information being continuously extracted from the individual, it should be feasible to deliver an amplified sense of personalized attention that is always relevant in addition to being delivered in a manner that is always compelling.

Developers must also keep in mind how the typical user interacts with the mobile phone platform. Whether having a voice telephony session, composing and sending a text message or browsing the web or watching a video, the typical user interaction with the mobile phone is usually measured in seconds or, at most, minutes. The virtual health assistant must be designed accordingly, or users will quickly abandon it. Interactions requiring long spans of attention won't work.

The typical user interaction with the mobile phone is usually measured in seconds or, at most, minutes. The virtual health assistant must be designed accordingly, or users will quickly abandon it.

It's also critical to keep in mind that interactions between the user and the virtual assistant might occur anywhere and at anytime—including in very public locations. Thus, in general, all interactions should be designed to be discreet, without sacrificing effectiveness. This is a significant implementation challenge that must be seriously considered, or the implementation will fail. No one wants their health status exposed to others.

Adding the Human Touch

The objective of the personal health assistant envisioned in this chapter is to provide tools directly to individuals, to enable them to self-manage a health condition (e.g., diabetes, obesity or cardiovascular disease) or maintain a state of wellness in order to avoid the onset of such conditions. At the end of the day, the task generally boils down to persuading individuals to change their behavior. Whether helping them to comply with their health provider's prescribed therapy or assisting them in avoiding destructive behavior, the personal health assistant must be able to "connect" with users in a way that is meaningful and compelling.

The mobile phone platform can enable an "always there," "always relevant" user experience, and careful design of the user interaction can help to make it meaningful and compelling. However, there is no substitute for human-to-human interaction when it comes to the subject of an individual's health and well being.

While a pure "live assistant" implementation is simply not affordable for a consumer offering, a live assistant component adds significant value. Coupled with the virtual assistant, the live assistant can result in the difference between achieving a compelling and affordable service offering or not. Again, the mobile phone is an ideal platform for delivering an integrated "virtual-live" personal health assistant implementation, given its ability to support both human-to-human and machine-to-machine interactions.

The Challenge of Reaching Consumers

Building effective and compelling health and wellness solutions around the cell phone platform will require the close collaboration of the wireless, medical device and health services industries. Such solutions can be introduced as "pure play" consumer offerings or as tools for augmenting the delivery of formal healthcare by the healthcare industry. The former can only be achieved if the solutions can be developed and delivered at a cost that permits them to be priced within the consumer's willingness to pay. In either case, the solutions must be compelling and effective or the individual will reject them—and the business model will fail.

About the Author

Paul Hedtke spent 17 years in the aerospace and military electronics industry in positions ranging from engineer, to engineering project management, to product management, to business development while working on a wide range of advanced aerospace and military electronics systems R&D projects. Paul joined QUALCOMM in 1998 and has served as project leader on numerous product and business development initiatives. He is currently leading a QUALCOMM strategic initiative to bring "health related" services to consumers using the cell phone platform as the primary user interface to such services.

Mobile Persuasion for Everyday Behavior Change

Sunny Consolvo, Member of Research Staff, Intel Research Seattle
Eric Paulos, Senior Research Scientist, Intel Research Berkeley
Ian Smith, Senior Member of Research Staff, Intel Research Seattle

Intel Research, the University of Washington, and the University of California, Berkeley are collaborating on the design and development of two mobile applications to persuade people to change their attitudes and behaviors in their everyday lives. The first application, UbiFit Garden, encourages people to live a healthy lifestyle by participating in regular physical activity. The basic idea is that a garden blooms on the screen background of an individual's mobile phone as she performs physical activities throughout the week. UbiFit Garden subtly conveys key information about the individual's behavior to improve her awareness of her level of physical activity and gently persuade her to participate in regular physical activity.

The second application, Environmental Awareness, transforms people's mobile devices into environmental measuring instruments that are outfitted with sensors to detect properties of air quality, such as carbon monoxide, sulfur dioxide, particulate matter, and ozone. Through these mobile measuring instruments, individuals receive instantaneous readings of the level of contaminants in their immediate environment. By sharing this data across large urban areas, citizens collectively generate real-time, detailed views of air quality across individual intersections, neighborhoods, parks, etc. Armed with increased awareness, Environmental Awareness seeks to motivate environmentally conscious change in an individual's behavior as well as within governmental policies.

These two different applications share high-level design strategies in the way that they attempt to motivate change in people's attitudes and behaviors.

First, both focus on offering the individual immediate, personal benefit to persuade them to use the applications initially. Second, through repeated use, the individual becomes aware of longer-term trends in behavior and gains a more accurate picture of how her daily behaviors impact her everyday life. Through this trend awareness, the applications seek to motivate sustainable behavior change.

Following is an overview of the key aspects of UbiFit Garden and Environmental Awareness.

> The applications use a similar approach to motivate change in people's attitudes and behaviors. Both offer immediate, personal benefit to persuade individuals to use the applications initially. Through repeated use, the individuals become aware of longer-term trends in their behavior and how their daily behavior impacts everyday life. Through this awareness, the applications seek to motivate sustainable behavior change.

UbiFit Garden

UbiFit Garden uses the screen background of an individual's mobile phone to display a garden that blooms as she performs physical activities throughout the week. Upon meeting her weekly goal, a butterfly appears. Smaller butterflies provide recent history, reminding her of goals she met for recent weeks (Figure 1).

UbiFit Garden uses positive reinforcement. If the individual is having an inactive week, she is not punished with wilting flowers or a stormy sky. Instead, she will simply see a sparse (or empty) garden with a blue sky and healthy grass (e.g., Figures 1a, 1b, & 1c).

Figure 1 UbiFit Garden background screen design. a) the garden at the beginning of the week; b) the garden at the beginning of the week with small, white butterflies to indicate goal achievement for the prior three weeks; c) after one workout; d) a garden with workout variety; e) an active week full of variety—the large butterfly indicates that the individual met her goal this week; f) active week with only one type of activity; g) the UbiFit Garden on a mobile phone. The small, white butterflies in b), d), & g) indicate that the individual met her goal for recent weeks.

To evaluate UbiFit Garden, we use fixed mappings for what the images in the garden represent. Different types of flowers represent different types of physical activities—specifically, cardiovascular, strength training, flexibility training, and walking. A large butterfly represents that this week's goal was met, and a small butterfly represents that a goal was met for a recent week (Figure 2). At a glance, the individual can determine if she is having a generally active or inactive week, if she has incorporated variety into her routine, if she has met her weekly goal, and if she has met her goal recently (Figure 1).

image	what it represents
	cardiovascular activity
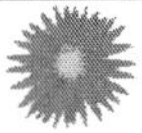	strength-training session
	flexibility training session
	walk
	this week's goal met
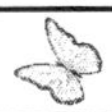	goal met for a prior week

Figure 2 Image mappings. The images in the garden represent different types of physical activities (e.g., cardio, strength, flexibility, and walking) and indicators regarding goal attainment. The variation of images gives the individual a sense of variety in her physical activities (e.g., is she doing lots of cardio but no strength training or does she have a well-balanced routine?).

Because UbiFit Garden runs on the background screen of the individual's phone, she is subtly reminded whenever and wherever she uses her phone of relevant information about her behavior. Given mobile phone usage frequency, this reminder should occur often enough to help the individual meet her goal or at least have an active week. It also provides a frequent but subtle reminder of her commitment to a physically active lifestyle.

The individual is unlikely to draw unwanted attention to herself when using UbiFit Garden, as it is common for people to use mobile phones in a wide range of settings. Further, because UbiFit Garden runs on her phone's background screen, the individual does not have to learn any new tasks to get relevant information about her physical activity.

Environmental Awareness

Environmental Awareness is a mobile phone application that uses an onboard carbon monoxide sensor and assisted GPS to measure and report the real-time air quality that an individual encounters. The data is uploaded *in situ* to a central, shared database where real-time air quality reports are generated and distributed to other mobile phone users. The novel hardware is a small scale, low-power (< 350 micro amps at 3 volts), micro fuel cell, carbon monoxide sensor (Figure 3).

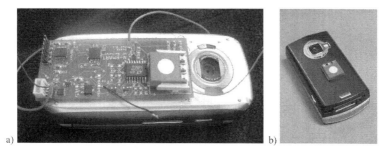

Figure 3 Sensor package on mobile phone. a) custom sensor board with carbon monoxide sensor (the carbon monoxide sensor is the square sensor with a white dot in the center, to left of camera lens) attached to the back of an LG VX9800 CDMA mobile phone; b) a more fully integrated envisioned design.

Environmental Awareness builds on the theme of Participatory Urbanism, whereby citizens act as agents of change. Presently, citizens must defer to a handful of civic government-installed, environmental monitoring stations that use extrapolation to derive a single air quality measurement for an entire metropolitan region. This sparse sensing method does little to capture the dynamic variability arising from daily automobile traffic patterns, human activity, and smaller industries (Figure 4). Integrating simple air quality sensors into networked mobile phones promotes everyday citizens to uncover, visualize, and collectively share real-time air quality measurements from their own everyday urban lives. This people-driven sensor data leverages community power imbalances and can increase agency and understanding of a community's claims, potentially increasing public trust. This detailed local knowledge informs environmental health research and policy making—motivating both individuals and civic governments to achieve positive improvements in air quality and environmental change.

Figure 4 Carbon monoxide readings across Accra, Ghana. Trails represent individual taxicabs, patch size indicates the intensity reading of carbon monoxide during a single day across the capital city of Ghana. Note the variation across the city and within small neighborhoods.

High-Level, Shared Design Strategies

Two high-level design strategies are employed by UbiFit Garden and Environmental Awareness to motivate initial use of the applications and encourage continued use over time.

Persuading Users to Get Started

Given that UbiFit Garden and Environmental Awareness are personal applications that will be used voluntarily by the individual (i.e., use will not be mandated by an employer, insurance company, etc.), we need to persuade the individual to *start using* the applications. Our strategy is to offer immediate, personal benefits. For instance, as soon as the user of UbiFit Garden does a workout, her garden begins to bloom, and the more physically active she is, the more attractive her garden becomes. Not only do the flowers and butterflies serve to convey relevant information about the individual's behavior, but they also serve as small "rewards" for performing healthy behaviors. In the case of Environmental Awareness, for the small cost of adding a few sensors to a device that the individual already carries, she receives meaningful, personal benefits of being able to monitor her current environment and receive alerts when she ventures into harmful atmospheric conditions.

Motivating Continued Use

Given that these applications attempt to motivate sustained behavior change in everyday life, they will likely need to be used over long periods of time to be effective. Therefore the applications must provide continued benefit to avoid falling victim to the "novelty effect" and subsequent abandonment.

Why would an individual continue to use UbiFit Garden or Environmental Awareness? Our strategy for answering that question is to provide the individual with key information to improve her awareness of trends in her behavior and realize the positive impact of behavior change on her everyday life.

In prior, related research using mobile phones, pedometers, and social influence to encourage an increase in daily step count, we found that some individuals have an unrealistic view of their actual levels of physical activity (e.g., some individuals thought of themselves as being physically active when they were simply busy). We also found that some individuals who struggle to maintain physical activity as part of their everyday lives often do not consider their past behavior when choosing what they will do today, for example. At a minimum, we hope that UbiFit Garden will help the individual become more aware of trends in her own actual behavior as it relates to her physical activity. However, our goal is to successfully persuade individuals to incorporate physical activity into their everyday lives, which should lead to benefits far beyond awareness of activity levels (e.g., increased energy, improved health, etc).

In the case of Environmental Awareness, again we want to show individuals patterns in their own behavior that otherwise may not be easy to discern. The air quality that an individual encounters varies by time of day, route and mode of travel, and time of year. Individuals are also able to compare the levels of air pollution they are exposed to daily with that of their friends, family, or other citizens, not only in their own metropolis but also in cities across the globe. We hope to promote continued use by bringing these environmental phenomena and patterns to the individual's attention.

Benefiting Society As a Whole

Previously, we suggested that we use a "what's in it for me?" approach in persuading individuals to begin and continue using our mobile applications. We also have a broader vision. This vision is not offered to "sell" individuals on the applications or merely offer a good "cover story" to our attempts at persuasion. Rather, we believe that individuals behaving in their own self interest when it comes to their physical activity and environment can benefit not only themselves but society as a whole.

If UbiFit Garden can persuade even a small part of the population to incorporate regular physical activity into their everyday lives, there is no doubt that society would benefit. Rates of sedentary lifestyles are skyrocketing, as are the costs associated with the myriad health problems to which they contribute. According to the U.S. Centers for Disease Control and Prevention, over five billion dollars in heart disease costs alone could be saved if only 10% of adults in the U.S. began a regular walking program.

Although one benefit of Environmental Awareness is a better informed polity, we favor a more scientific argument. Thousands of individuals carrying "measuring instruments" at all times is a terrific way to collect scientific data. If this data were shared with scientists, understanding of the planet's atmosphere could be significantly increased through research on this aggregate data set.

> **Thousands of individuals carrying mobile measurement instruments at all times is a terrific way to collect scientific data. If this data were shared with scientists, understanding of the planet's atmosphere could be significantly increased through research on the aggregate data set.**

For example, the entire San Francisco Bay Area has a few dozen monitoring stations that collect samples of air quality and publish it at intervals of a few hours. If 1% of the Bay Area's ten million inhabitants were to carry a mobile atmospheric measuring instrument (e.g., their mobile phones) with them and upload the data they collect to a repository, it seems likely that this data set would quickly surpass the currently employed, fixed monitoring stations in terms of quality. At a minimum, this collaborative data would allow scientists to investigate phenomena at a far finer granularity than is currently possible.

Conclusion

Mobile technology has rapidly become intimately interwoven into our everyday lives. Our mobile devices go wherever we go and can easily begin to measure our daily experiences. As such, they can provide us with insights into understanding the habits and environmental exposures that are harmful to our health and well being. Using simple, novel tools and applications such as UbiFit Garden and Environmental Awareness, our mobile devices will begin to play an important role in persuading us not only to change individual decisions and behaviors, but in promoting a dialogue about issues such as health, fitness, and environmental air quality at a global level.

About the Authors

Sunny Consolvo joined Intel Research Seattle in 2001. She is also a Ph.D. candidate at the University of Washington's Information School. Sunny's research focuses on applying user-centered design to ubiquitous computing. In particular, she is interested in the social implications of ubiquitous computing technologies. Her current focus is on developing persuasive technologies to encourage people to incorporate regular physical activity into their everyday lives. Her prior research has included investigating privacy implications of location-enhanced technologies and developing technologies to help elders age in place. Sunny previously worked in Silicon Valley, where her focus was on web design and usability.

Ian Smith joined the Intel Research Seattle laboratory in 2003 where he explores the intersection of software technology and new experiences for mobile devices. Previously on staff at the Xerox Palo Alto Research Center (PARC), Ian focused on the integration of software development tools and practices with ethnographic techniques in user interface development. He was granted a Ph.D. in computer science from the Georgia Institute of Technology in 1998.

Eric Paulos is a senior research scientist at Intel in Berkeley, California where he leads the Urban Atmospheres project, which challenges him and his colleagues to use innovative methods to understand society and the future fabric of our emerging digital and wireless public urban landscapes and lifestyles. Eric's research interests span a deep body of work in urban computing, social telepresence, robotics, tangible media, and intimate computing. Eric received his Ph.D. in EECS from UC Berkeley where he researched scientific and social issues surrounding internet-based telepresence, robotics, and mediated communication tools. During that time he developed several internet-based tele-operated robots including, Personal Roving Presence devices (PRoPs) and Space Browsing helium-filled tele-operated blimps.

Acknowledgements

We would like to thank our friends and colleagues who have contributed to this work, in particular: Dr. Patrick Baudisch, Hooria Bittlingmayer, Professor Gaetano Borriello, Dr. Mike Chen, Dr. Tanzeem Choudhury, Kieran Del Pasqua, Dean Eckles, Kate Everitt, Cherie Fenner, Dr. B.J. Fogg, Jon Froehlich, Professor Steve Gribble, Dr. Beverly Harrison, RJ Honicky, Ben Hooker, Pedja Klasnja, Professor James Landay, Dr. Anthony LaMarca, Louis Legrand, Jonathan Lester, Ryan Libby, Professor David McDonald, Dr. Jean Moran, Dimitri Negroponte, Tammy Toscos, Professor David Wetherall, Alex Wilkie, and many others.

Design Insights

Perspective 11

Designing Engaging Mobile Experiences

Josh Ulm, Director of Experience Design, Mobile, Platform and Dynamic Media, Adobe Systems

Introduction

Mobile devices have become a direct extension of our eyes, ears, voice and mind. They have become our constant companions. We rely on them to stay in touch, guide our activities and entertain us. They have evolved from merely functional tools. Simple voice and data services are no longer sufficient. We have much greater expectations now.

To meet those expectations, a new class of mobile service is emerging, called *engaging mobile experiences*. These mobile experiences focus on the user. They prioritize usability, offer new services and deliver content instantaneously. More importantly, they build a powerful affinity with the user. They promise experiences that are expressive, memorable and much more desirable.

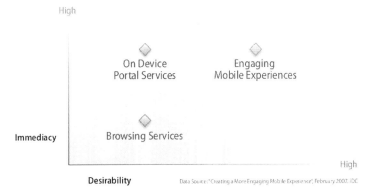

Figure 1 Desirability and immediacy combine to create engaging mobile experiences.

That promise, however, can only be met if the delivery recognizes the unique characteristics of the mobile user. Just as the rules for designing experiences changed when we moved from print to the web, designing for mobile has its own rules.

Creating Engaging Experiences: Three Principles

In the mobile space, devices are very different from desktop computers. Users are constantly on the move, often multitasking, and interacting in very social situations. Their attention is the most valuable commodity, and seducing them to stay connected is the ultimate goal. With that in mind, the following principles will be critical to creating the most persuasive and engaging mobile experiences.

Principle 1: The Mobile Context Is Relevant

Today's mobile phones try to be smaller versions of their desktop brethren. They have little lists and grids. Little web browsers. Little calendars. They assume that users do the same things on their phones that they do at their desks, and that the same interfaces are appropriate. They are not.

Mobile experiences should not only be smaller, they should be smarter. They must recognize the context and manner of mobile interactions and offer experiences that are appropriate for mobile.

Figure 2 *Not your father's desktop. Mobile experiences are all about being a mobile user. We are on the move. We are individuals, yet we want to stay connected. And we're hungry for stimulation.*

Focus on the User, Not the Technology

Today's mobile experiences tend to focus on technology, such as Push to Talk, Ringback Tones and WAP. Engaging mobile experiences are more valuable because they enable designers to emphasize users over features. Whether a mobile experience is intended for work or entertainment, it must go beyond merely being usable. To be engaging, it also should be dependable, consistently solve users' problems, and do so effortlessly. When designed properly, these experiences understand the task, the environment and the audience. They recognize that less is often more, and that just because you can, doesn't mean you should.

Design around Space Limitations

Space is extremely precious on mobile devices. If onscreen affordance doesn't help communicate how users will interact with the content and interface, it is a barrier to them. Mobile experiences are most valuable when they are straightforward and clearly represent their purpose. The presentation as a whole should be designed to be read and understood at a glance. Superfluous material should be avoided. Icons should be bold and simple. Text should be large, readable and digestible. Items should be spaced distinctly, such that relationships are clear and obvious. Data and information should be lightweight, network friendly and presented in small, relevant bits.

Use the Right Tools

Designing and developing great mobile experiences is impossible without specialized developer tools. In a painfully fragmented software landscape, it is critical that the development suite brings all the pieces back together. Mobile developer tools must recognize the creative needs of designers, yet be familiar and empowering to software designers and developers. More importantly, the tools must integrate seamlessly to allow both roles to work together. To address an ever-changing sea of devices, mobile tools also must be able to emulate hardware capabilities and provide for accurate testing. They must be flexible, yet offer precise control. Subsequently, they must be powerful and capable of unleashing the best aspects of the mobile phone.

Principle 2: Capturing and Guiding Users Is Essential

Mobile users are subject to countless distractions and technology disadvantages. Screens are small, environments are noisy and networks are undependable. Hardware is always a barrier; users must struggle with tiny keyboards and screens. Software is often inconsistent, where every application, device and carrier solves the same problems in radically different ways.

Great mobile experiences overcome these barriers by recognizing them and addressing them directly. They do so by establishing a clear focus, direction and emphasis; maintaining context throughout the user experience; and enabling users to preview the results of each action they consider taking.

Figure 3 When everything is equal, nothing is important. Techniques like animation and expanding focus draw emphasis to the item of attention.

Establish Clear Focus, Direction and Emphasis

Mobile experiences depend on the success of the user being able to find the object of focus quickly and easily despite distractions. User focus should be implemented in a simple, clear and consistent way across interfaces. Actions should be intuitive and natural. Users shouldn't have to think hard about what options are available to them.

Hardware can help in this area. Consider taking advantage of the 5-way navigation key and keypad by mapping key presses to actions with spatial and directional significance. The interaction required by the UI should be both visually and reflexively intuitive to the user.

Maintain Context

As users navigate mobile experiences, it is critical that they are able to recognize where they are and what they can do. Moving from screen to screen can be disorienting if the context changes radically or often. Maintain context by expanding the view of content in place instead of jumping between pages. Use animation to help reinforce physical interactions, display new functionality and content, and ease dramatic changes in context. As much as possible, keep interaction models consistent, even when the content switches between very different tasks. While it is inevitable that users will have to learn new interaction patterns, they will be more successful when they are able to leverage their experience and knowledge of previous interactions as they find new ones.

Preview and Deliver

Taking the wrong action can ruin an experience. Ideally, users should have a sense of the result of an action before they commit to it. Previews are a valuable tool for helping users determine what to expect. In the best case, previews can even supplant the need to take further action at all. Surfacing information in a contextual manner will help users to make effective, efficient decisions. Once a decision is made, it is equally important to support a strong sense of response and offer immediate feedback to the user. Engaging experiences must be fast, responsive and unmistakable.

Principle 3: Differentiation Is a Feature

Engaging mobile experiences are ones that stand out from the crowd. They should make us stand out from the crowd as well. More and more, mobile devices represent identity—from how they look to how they are used. The experiences they deliver must be rich, compelling and connect personally to users. They should be exciting, fun and desirable. To make mobile users stand out from the crowd, developers must focus on style, brand experiences and personalization. They must provide a thrill to users, and deliver experiences that are fresh and dynamic.

Figure 4 Mobile phones are often seen as a reflection of personal identity. The visual design should be complementary, pleasing and even fashionable.

Make it Stylish

The idea of engaging mobile experiences challenges the notion that mobile devices are mere tools. Phones have increasingly become a reflection of individuals' affiliations, purpose and personality—even their status in society. So for many mobile users, style can trump features. To be engaging, mobile experiences must be fashionable. They must make a statement and offer users a broad palette to express themselves in unique, beautiful and arresting ways.

Demonstrate Brand

Mobile users are ready and willing to engage with their favorite brands on their phones. Mobile experiences that can faithfully represent brands will be more engaging for users who are hungry for authentic experiences. Whether brands choose to partner with carriers or distributors to reach mobile customers or decide to go it alone, they are choosing to deliver experiences that recognize the value of their brand rather than having their content repurposed in ways that might dilute their integrity.

Customize Deeply

One size of mobile experience does not fit all. While personalization is not new, downloadable ringtones and backgrounds are no longer enough. Users are demanding much more than simple aesthetic customization. Services and features must be available on demand. Engaging experiences must deliver tailored content and subscriptions, enable personalized work flows and surface essential functionality. However, to be successful they must do all of this without requiring users to invest great effort. Ultimately, they must recognize our individual needs and learn our behaviors; even adapt and grow. Engaging mobile experiences must come alive.

Give Users a Thrill

It's not enough for mobile experiences to be good; they must be exceptional. Surging competition among services demands that mobile experiences are desirable in order to be engaging. As consumers, we are hungry for the next great experience—for new experiences that are fun, popular and memorable. Our phones keep us connected to our community and we are eager to have experiences that we can share with friends and family. Today, mobile experiences only hint at that potential. Engaging mobile experiences will deliver on the promise that they can be truly thrilling.

Keep it Fresh and Dynamic

The mobile user's attention span is a fragile commodity, easily lost if not stimulated. Network latency is a significant barrier between users and content. Engaging mobile content is consumed rapidly and with great frequency; therefore, it must be timely and relevant, immediately available and easily accessible. However, simply making sure content is available is not enough. Mobile content cannot be flat and boring. On the contrary, it must make use of rich media, video, audio, high-fidelity graphics and animation to captivate, excite and entertain.

Conclusion

As consumers, our hunger for engaging mobile experiences is undeniable. Already in the marketplace a battle is waging for our attention. The providers who will come out on top will be the ones who are the most persuasive—the ones who embrace this new model of seductive mobile experience design. However, the real winners will be mobile users. A new buffet of experiences is being prepared just for us. And it will be a feast.

About the Author

Josh Ulm is Director of Experience Design for Mobile, Platform and Dynamic Media at Adobe Systems, Inc. Since joining Macromedia in 2004 and continuing with Adobe, he has worked predominately with Mobile and Devices to define the mobile experience platform, and he works directly with developers and customers to create engaging Flash Lite experiences. His work has driven the successful adoption of many products and technologies for the combined companies and their customers; he is frequently asked to develop and present the company's experience vision; and he is an active and respected veteran within the Flash and mobile developer communities.

Perspective 12

The Four Pillars of a Successful Mobile Marketing Vision

Eric Holmen, President, SmartReply, Inc.

Unlike some fun applications of mobile technology, mobile *marketing* has the potential to make the mobile phone experience miserable. The mobile phone is different from other advertising-enriched technologies, such as radio, television and the internet, because mobile communications are highly personal. The advertiser has little understanding of the recipient's environment when the message is delivered. With TV advertising or internet ads, marketers can be fairly certain that people are sitting down and engaged with their content. That's not the case with mobile phone ads. But there's good news: When done well, mobile marketing can offer value to both advertisers and recipients.

For instance, one of my company's clients found a win-win solution in a mobile marketing campaign during the summer of 2006. At that time gasoline prices had risen to record levels; in some areas, prices had increased 80% in a matter of a few months. Of course, consumers were not happy. This trend was a problem for our client, Meijer Supercenters, which operated gas stations in the parking lots of their superstores.

To keep their customers happy, Meijer launched an innovative solution. The company set up a simple and important mobile messaging alert system. Prior to a gas price increase (which was not under Meijer's control), Meijer would send an alert to all interested customers, allowing them four to six hours to fill up their tanks before the price on the pumps was updated. This was a simple, valuable alignment of content and context.

Customers felt in control with Meijer on their side. And Meijer benefited in other ways. As customers stopped in to top off their gas tanks (thank you,

Meijer!), they also grabbed fixings for dinner or a new sweatshirt. Value, it seems, is contagious from the parking lot to the store shelves.

Messaging on mobile phones seems simple. Each message can have 160 characters. How complicated can that be? Very complicated, as SmartReply has learned. However, we've found that the complexity lies in the relationship with the consumer, not in the medium itself.

The Four Pillars

To help navigate the complexity involved in creating successful mobile marketing campaigns, my team has outlined what we call our "four pillars" of a mobile marketing vision:

- Consumer preference is a sovereign right.
- Great marketing is a service.
- Personalization is critical.
- Relationships drive transactions.

Consumer Preference Is a Sovereign Right

The successful mobile marketer starts with the premise that any customer interaction is an engagement. Customers are clients, deserving of respect for their intellect, their needs, and their preferences. The mobile phone is the most personal of technologies, and consumers are protective of how their phones get used. Customers must be able to engage and disengage at will, via text, WAP, internet, a phone call, a visit to the store, an email, etc. When it comes to mobile phones, customers are the monarchs and high rulers of their advertising experience fiefdom. Advertisers who do not honor that sovereignty will eventually be banished.

Great Marketing Is a Service

Mobile marketing can provide customers a valuable service. Meijer's text messaging of gas price increases to its customers is a great example.

But the possibilities go beyond text messaging. Text has a sexier sister: multimedia messaging or MMS. This technology allows marketers to send pictures, barcodes, short videos, and other images. With MMS, the marketing possibilities expand, along with the potential to provide richer, more persuasive service experiences to customers.

For example, imagine that you're in the fresh fish department of your favorite grocery store. You see so many choices, you don't know what to bring home for dinner. At this moment of need, you could request a video MMS message to your phone, in which cooking show host Rachael Ray demonstrates how to prepare fresh salmon with cheesy potatoes. You think "Perfect!" When you arrive home with fresh salmon and a new recipe to boot, you're the family hero.

Marketers can provide even richer services when their customers download applications for their mobile phones. For example, a building supply company could create a mobile application for construction contractors. This could help them calculate board-feet for a project, search a few local yards for the lumber, and confirm the order and delivery information. The application could even allow the customer to barter for goods and services. Such an application would help build customer loyalty.

Personalization Is Critical

At SmartReply, we know that personalization is critical in mobile marketing. We learned this lesson the hard way. In an early client project, we sent 750,000 mobile messages to customers who had signed up for mobile alerts as part of the client's loyalty program. We were delighted by the initial response: 83% of the messages were opened within an hour. This led to an 834% increase in incremental sales. Everyone was happy until a month later, when we repeated the campaign and the response rate was terrible. So what happened?

After some investigation, we determined why the repeat campaign had failed—or, more importantly, why the initial campaign had worked so well. When customers received the first text message, this was novel, so the client's message stood out. The second message was no longer novel, and felt like old news to customers (because it was).

We've learned that to keep response rates high, we must personalize messages. In the case of our client's campaign, we came up with a new mobile marketing strategy that involved segmenting customers according to their purchases and targeting a different message to each segment. Customers

---

The Four Pillars of Successful Mobile Marketing

1. **Consumer preference is a sovereign right.** Consumers are protective of how their phones get used. They must be able to engage and disengage at will, via text, WAP, internet, a phone call, store visit, or other means. Advertisers who do not honor consumers' preferences will eventually be banished.

2. **Great marketing is a service.** Mobile marketing can provide customers valuable services, via text or multimedia messaging (MMS). For instance, text messaging could be used to notify customers of price increases or product discounts. MMS could be used to help customers complete a task, such as cooking a meal with products purchased at the marketer's store. Such services can inspire customer loyalty.

3. **Personalization is critical.** Customers may respond to any mobile marketing campaign only once, simply due to its novelty. To achieve results over time, however, requires personalizing the message. For instance, customers who bought Brand A might receive news about Brand A, those buying Brand B would get discounts on Brand B, and so on. Such a targeted strategy can increase the number of customer transactions.

4. **Relationships drive transactions.** Mobile marketing in and of itself does not drive business transactions. Relationships do. In contrast to marketing via other media, such as TV and newsprint, mobile marketing campaigns may not generate immediate spikes in transactions. Rather, developing successful, engaging relationships with customers leads to a greater number of transactions over time.

---

who bought Brand A would receive news about Brand A, those buying Brand B would get discounts on Brand B, and so on. In addition, rather than measuring results on a campaign-by-campaign basis, we began looking at purchase cycle activity, with the goal of driving an incremental purchase each year, for each customer. Though we are still measuring the results, it looks like this goal will be easily achieved.

Even though the idea of personalization seems obvious, few mobile marketing campaigns tailor their messages to the customer's interests in this way. But we've learned that doing so is critical to success, and that it creates ongoing value.

Relationships Drive Transactions

Marketing in and of itself does not drive business transactions. Relationships do. More specifically, successful and engaging relationships will lead to a greater number of transactions over time.

This statement may seem somewhat obvious today, but in the past this lesson apparently was not obvious to traditional marketers. They were accustomed to the immediate spikes in business that followed TV and newsprint campaigns. Today the growth of interactive marketing—especially on the mobile platform—highlights how much success depends on developing the relationship between the brand and the customer.

How do you develop this relationship? The answer is found in the first three pillars of a successful mobile marketing vision. In brief, brands need to provide their customers with valuable services, personalized for each customer, and delivered in a way that respects the customer's wishes.

Summary

Almost daily someone asks us this question: "How urgent is it for me to launch a mobile initiative?" At SmartReply, we answer as follows: If your competitor succeeds in engaging your customer before you do, then your job becomes much harder, if not impossible.

Of course, speed is not the only issue. In the near term, quick-and-dirty mobile marketing campaigns will work. Because receiving ads on a mobile phone is still novel, people respond to them. Once. However, the ongoing prospects for this approach are not good; such an approach will appeal only to the discount shoppers who have no loyalty to brands.

We encourage our clients to see the bigger picture of which customer types will create real value for their businesses. We've found that discount-driven customers are not the most profitable in the long run. The customers with brand loyalty can generate 70% of the profit margin. These valuable customers only welcome mobile marketing messages that are relationship driven. They tend to blacklist most other types of communications to their mobile phones.

Advertising, as they say, is all about the sizzle, not about the steak. As companies craft their plans for a mobile-marketing strategy, they would be wise to avoid the pitfalls of advertising sizzle. While TV and radio excel in delivering an enticing brand promise, the mobile platform is uniquely positioned to transform the brand promise into a concrete reality.

About the Author

Eric Holmen brings extensive experience to SmartReply, with a diverse retail marketing background that includes strategic planning; marketing; sales and operational management; and strategic partnerships for many leading companies, including Sears, Roebuck, & Co. and Catalina Marketing. He developed a reputation for innovation and experimentation in each role and has been awarded several patents and global awards.

Eric received his undergraduate degree in management science from the University of Redlands, is married with three children and lives in Orange County, California. "We're excited to be on the leading edge of reshaping how our nation, and maybe the world, markets with their consumers."

Pervasive Persuasive Play: Rhetorical Game Design for the Ubicomp World

Steffen P. Walz, Chair for Computer Aided Architectural Design, ETH Zurich

In the era of ubiquitous computing, the persuasive nature and potential of pervasive games empowers designers and entrepreneurs to create experiences that enthrall, inspire, and influence mobile audiences. Games are, by their nature, rhetorical. They captivate their audience and intrinsically motivate players so that they start playing and are persuaded to keep playing (Walz 2003). Game designers—regardless of whether they create a board game or console product—avail themselves of persuasion tactics to achieve this immersive, often *flow-like* interactive experience for their players.

A fundamental persuasion tactic that game designers apply is a *reward*. Rewards encourage players to remain in the game. A *long-term* reward is the ultimate form of a reward in a game. Usually, this type of reward is initiated by and coupled with a promise.

> Games create interactions that captivate their audience and intrinsically motivate players so that they start playing and are persuaded to keep playing. Game designers apply persuasion tactics to achieve this immersive, often *flow-like* experience for their players.

For example, the promise may be that if you keep jumping over rolling barrels, continue running and climbing up ladders across four levels without fail, you will not only win this game but you will also save your girlfriend—and therefore the (game) world, from the scheming evil gorilla who has kidnapped her. The role and gender assignation in *Donkey Kong,* whose gameplay I described in the above example, may appeal predominantly to a teenage, heterosexual, male audience and the scenario may appear banal. Yet, something as mundane as saving a game's world can be highly persuasive: Rewards induce learning, and learning in turn induces a persistent and positive, effective, cognitive and intentional state of mind in a player:

"Fun in games arises out of mastery," writes Raph Koster, the lead designer of the massively multiplayer role-playing game *Ultima Online*. "It arises out of comprehension. It is the act of solving puzzles that makes games fun. In other words, with games, learning is the drug." (Koster 2005).

Games Move Beyond the Desktop

At the beginning of the 21st century, digital games are no longer bound to the desktop computer. Instead, everyday objects and physical environments with invisible and networked computing functionality assist to "extend the gaming experience out into the real world—be it on city streets, in the remote wilderness, or a living room" (Benford et al. 2004). With this growing pervasiveness of computing, the implicit persuasive nature of games unfolds regardless, or because of, the player's geographical and social context. In the ubicomp world, the game is where we are, and the space we occupy can temporarily or permanently turn into a "playce" wherein a designer can influence the player's mobility, decision-making and emotions to a certain extent.

One example of such a playcemaking game is REXplorer, a project my team at the ETH Zurich and I cocreated with Rafael "Tico" Ballagas and his team from RWTH Aachen University's Media Computing Group (Walz et al. 2006).

> Digital games are no longer bound to the desktop computer. Instead, everyday objects and physical environments with invisible and networked computing functionality assist to "extend the gaming experience out into the real world." In this world, a game designer can influence a player's mobility, decision making and emotions to a certain extent.

REXplorer is a location-based pervasive game service that targets day tripping tourists visiting the medieval, UNESCO protected city core of Regensburg, Germany. The players, "REXplorers", cast "spells" at city sights using a gesture-recognizing rental game controller, a shell housing a smartphone and a GPS receiver. Casting the proper, site-specific gesture spell in the fashion of moving a *Nintendo Wiimote* through the air (see Figure 1) rewards the player with the evocation of a typical Regensburg character, who speaks to the player through the game controller.

Figure 1 Casting the gesture-based spell "wind" with the REXplorer controller evokes a character.

This character—for example, the mythological architect of the Regensburg cathedral—tells the player a cliff-hanging story. In their stories, characters hint at the gesture the player must use in order to accept a quest assignment. This assignment reveals at which of the other 28 game sites in the city the player can resolve the quest, score points for its completion and listen to the closure of the cliff-hanger—after which the player will be offered the next quest.

The sites are interconnected; the oft-branching quests create a network of spatial location links, thereby mapping the mechanics, and mobility inducing patterns of many computer games, onto the physical world. For the player, a new mental map of a playce comes alive (see Figure 2).

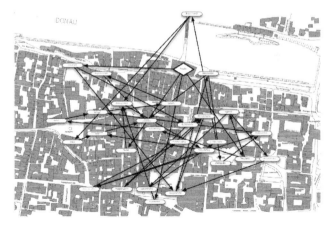

Figure 2 Map of Regensburg's city core with character sites and a character quest network.

The Explicit Persuasive Potential of Games

How can ubicomp games be persuasive beyond their implicit rhetorical nature, which already turns the world into an ever-gratifying, magical playground rich with spatially linked locations and objects—*stuff* ready to be toyed with, a playce ready to be mastered? Is an "enchanted village", propagated by ubicomp pioneer Rich Gold in 1993, even desirable? An enchanted ubicomp setting not only grants the player agency; it also must, in varying degrees, control or surveil the player in order to guarantee an optimal experience. This has ethical, legal and liability consequences that designers of these types of experiences need to consider.

"Serious games" aim at inspiring, educating, and training their audiences beyond mere entertainment. These digital games exhibit rhetorical qualities *explicitly*, and can be thought of as examples of persuasive technologies, i.e., "interactive computing products created for the purpose of changing people's attitudes or behaviors" (Fogg 2003).

> **"Serious games" aim at inspiring and educating audiences beyond mere entertainment. For instance, a tourism game could help visitors to engage with and learn about the history and culture of their destination. Such games are examples of persuasive technologies, created for the purpose of changing people's attitudes or behaviors.**

REXplorer applies the serious game concept to the domain of tourism, helping visitors to engage with and, most importantly, to learn about the history and culture of their destination in an innovative, computer game-like way. One example of an explicit persuasion tactic is the souvenir weblog. In REXplorer the player may take pictures with the rental game controller, which, together with descriptions of the characters encountered, are uploaded to the player's personalized souvenir weblog. This souvenir weblog also depicts the players' actual route through the city (see Figure 3). Both implicitly and explicitly, we can think of REXplorer as an example of a pervasive persuasive game.

I believe that pervasive persuasive games can be a valuable product beyond mere experimentation, for educational, military, health related, policy-making, or social and political purposes. Projects such as REXplorer prove this, at least for the tourism and marketing sector.

Figure 3 A personalized weblog with the player's gameplay session as a "souvenir."

Design Dimensions of Pervasive Persuasive Games

What are the starting points for designing your own pervasive persuasive games, for creating playces for your players? I believe that four dimensions require equal consideration at the beginning of a game development project. Note that these design dimensions are not isolated, but impact one another:

- The player

- The place to play

- The technology

- The game

The Player

Knowing and understanding the audience is central to designing any media content. In games, the player is central. Typical questions in the beginning of a project include

- What is the typical *player's background?* How would you describe the player—a competitor, a contemplator, a strategist, a socializer, etc.? What kind of medial and technological expertise does the player bring to the game?

- What are the *player's primary and secondary activities* before, during and after the expected game situation? What are the player's motives for being where he or she is and what he or she does outside of the game? How will the game change this?

- *Where* is the player, and how does she or he move about? At what pace? What is the activity space of the player in her or his current *place*?

- What are potential *concerns* the player may have with regards to playing? What is the player's "gameness", including allotted time, budget, theatricality, and constraints?

- (When) Does the player have *company*?

The Place to Play

The less public a place, and the more specific the place, the easier it will be to turn it into a playce, as it becomes controllable. The more a place has been designed specifically for your game, the better, and the less you have to design your game to suit the place. Among the many questions that can help you understand the place, or places, you plan to use for your game are the following:

- What is the *mediality* of the place? Is it, for example, a book, a website, or a built environment?

- What is the *architecture* of the place, including its ontology, topology, geometry, and reality; its layout, visibility, ensemble, relation to the surroundings, and psychogeographical type (e.g. castle; prison; market plaza)? Is it mobile? Is it a dynamic space? Do environmental conditions play a role? Is it software or hardware?

- What is the *stageability* of the place—what are its affordances, what is its atmosphere like, next to its sensorial qualities, its navigability, its travelability, its current, past, and future usages? Is it crowded? Trafficked? When? What are the constraints of the place? Is it exclusive? How does one get there, how does one leave? How much effort does it require to traverse the place?

- *How many places* does the game involve? How are they connected?

The Technology

The field of ubiquitous computing seeks to equip everyday objects and physical environments with networked computing functionality that is often invisible. Questions to determine the initial technological requirements of your pervasive persuasive game include the following:

- What is the *technological infrastructure* at hand, including affordances, budget, accessibility, connectivity, accuracy, serendipity, synchronicity, runtime, sequentiality / continuity, servicing, fidelity, etc.?

- What *technological infrastructure* is afforded by your *player* in the context of the specific *place(s)* and *game?*

The Game

Following are select questions that support your understanding and balancing of the elements your game consists of, and how these affect the player, the place(s) and the technology you plan to use:

- What are the *formal elements* of the game—how do its rules and conflict(s), its objectives and reward structure and its player interactions and procedures interplay with what you know about the player, the place for play and the technology you will be using?

- What are the *dramaturgical elements* of the game—how do its premise, its story and dramatic arc, its narrative and gameplay challenges and emotionality, and lastly its characters relate to the player, the place and your technology?

Conclusion

I have highlighted the persuasive nature and the persuasive potential of pervasive games, introducing starting points for the design of your own projects. Let us make sure to use the power of pervasive persuasive games ethically, in the spirit of the Ciceronian ideal of the *orator perfectus,* who is, naturally, a *vir bonus*—a good (hu)man.

About the Author

Steffen P. Walz, M.A. is an award-winning game designer and researcher who is currently working on his Ph.D. thesis on the design rhetoric of pervasive and mobile games at the ETH Zurich in Switzerland.

As of 2007, Steffen is a Forum Nokia Champion and Birkhäuser Basel Boston Berlin is publishing the book *Space Time Play: Synergies between Computer Games, Architecture and Urbanism,* which was co-edited by Steffen.

Since 2000, his firm playbe has been consulting for web and design enterprises and institutions concerned with persuasive media endeavors. A complete list of Steffen's activities can be found at his website playbe's place at http://spw.playbe.com.

Citations

Benford, S., Magerkurth, C. & Ljungstrand, P. (2005). "Bridging the Physical and Digital in Pervasive Gaming" *Communications of the ACM* 48(3): 54–58.

Fogg, B.J. (2003). *Persuasive Technology: Using Computers to Change What We Think and Do.* San Francisco, CA, Morgan Kaufmann.

Gold, R. (1993). "This Is Not a Pipe." Communications of the ACM 36(7): 72.

Koster, R. (2005). A Theory of Fun for Game Design. Scottsdale, AZ, Paraglyph Press.

Walz, Steffen P. (2003). "Delightful Identification & Persuasion: Towards an Analytical and Applied Rhetoric of Digital Games" in Copier, M. & Raessens, J. (eds.). *Level Up. Proceedings of the 1st International Digital Games Research Conference.* Utrecht, University of Utrecht Press and DiGRA: 194–207.

Walz, S.P. et al. (2006). "Cell Spell-Casting: Designing a Locative and Gesture Recognition Multiplayer Smartphone Game for Tourists" in Strang, T., Cahill, C. & Quigley, A. (eds.): Pervasive 2006 Workshop Proceedings. Dublin, University College Press: 149–156.

Perspective 14

Mobile Persuasion and the Power of Meaning

George LeBrun, President and CEO, Rule 13

If companies fail to gain the attention of consumers, they will not have the opportunity to persuade them. Unfortunately, due to information overload and the demands of everyday life in the 21st century, the attention of consumers has become a scarce commodity. Thanks to the internet, which offers an almost infinite number of channels of content, getting and holding consumers' attention has become more difficult than ever. Those companies that do manage to win consumers' attention face another challenge: persuading them to change their behavior, which is, and always has been, difficult.

We are seeing companies grapple with these challenges in the mobile arena. For instance, advertisers are struggling with how to entice consumers to watch ads on mobile phones. Furthermore, paying and waiting for the download of content hasn't caught on with mobile users in the way that Hollywood and traditional advertisers anticipated it would.[1]

The Customer Persuasion Process[2]

One reason why companies have largely failed to win the attention of mobile consumers is that they are focused on the technology rather than the human needs that it fulfills. To get consumers' attention and succeed in persuading them to purchase new products and services, companies must focus on triggering meaning. Services and products that are meaningful to mobile users have a far greater chance of being noticed and adopted.

Triggering Meaning

Phones, email, telephony, and other forms of communication are often referred to as "killer apps" because they have such a deep impact on and popularity with customers. However, the reason for this is often overlooked. Communications media are highly popular because they engage us on levels much deeper and more meaningful than simply price and performance.

Persuasion, too, operates on a deeper level. In order for persuasive experiences to be successful, they must be meaningful. And the more meaningful they are, the more engaging and valuable they are to us.

It is far easier to persuade consumers to engage with mobile services and products by triggering meaning than by simply advertising product features and price. For instance, MySpace became wildly successful because consumers found it highly meaningful to their lives, not as the result of a big-budget advertising campaign.

The mobile experiences that companies create must be powerful enough to evoke meaning for customers. For example, by responding to and joining cause-based programs, such as environmental or political programs, companies can gain the immediate loyalty of consumers who support the same cause. In this way, they have successfully triggered meaning with those consumers, who will now become not only users, but evangelists for the brand.

> Communications media are highly popular because they engage us on levels much deeper and more meaningful than simply price and performance. Similarly, mobile services and products that are meaningful to users will have a far greater chance of being noticed and adopted.

Addressing Maslow's Hierarchy of Needs

How can companies determine what is meaningful to consumers, so they can provide relevant mobile services and products? Maslow's hierarchy of needs provides a powerful model (Figure 1). Companies that deliver services and products that meet the needs identified in Maslow's hierarchy will be more successful in persuading consumers to engage with them.

The basic psychological needs Maslow defined, such as food, warmth, and comfort, correspond to basic mobile services such as voice and text. Safety and security needs—the next level of the hierarchy—correspond to services like child tracking and security monitoring. The needs for *social belonging* and *love* could be met by services such as mobile dating, flirting via text messaging, and a range of community services. The need for esteem is met through the personalization of mobile devices. Finally, self-actualization needs, at the pinnacle of the hierarchy, are being met through the creation of content by users (Jaokar & Fish 2006).

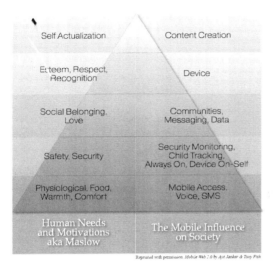

Figure 1 Maslow's hierarchy of needs, mapped against mobile services that could meet those needs (Jaokar & Fish 2006).

Companies that are able to design products and services that meet the emotional needs set forth by Maslow will find it easier to pierce the walled gardens created by mobile users. In addition, companies that can accomplish this effectively offline as well as on the mobile platform have a significantly better chance of succeeding. For example, a home security company offering a GPS application that could be installed onto any handset, regardless of its operating system and carrier, and which could pinpoint the location of children 24/7 and alert parents when the child returned home, would strike a sharp chord with adults who are concerned about the safety and security of their children.

Another example is Build-A-Bear Workshop®, a company that has driven growth and success by delivering experiences that trigger deep meaning for young girls across the country. By creating an assembly line environment, where customers choose an "unstuffed" bear, place a plastic heart inside their bear, which is then stuffed, sewn, dressed, and given a birth certificate, customers are engrossed in the experience of bringing their bear to life.

Build-a-Bear Workshop is very proactive in sending emails to customers announcing upcoming additions to its stores. Since the company has done an incredible job in triggering meaning in its customer base, if it were to create a mobile community and add mobile messaging to deliver customer updates, it could continue to meet the emotional needs of *social belonging* and *love* through its mobile offerings.

For some mobile users, Maslow's highest need, *self actualization,* is already being met. For instance, there are many examples of mobile phone users capturing photos and video on the scene of a newsworthy event, and later seeing those photos and videos broadcast nationwide. The innate ability of mobile devices to empower ordinary consumers in a way that could land them in the national spotlight is highly fulfilling.

Customer Persuasion Process

1. Business Rules Assessment
2. Customer Innovation Insight
3. Customer Experience Design
   Delivering Experience
   Think Sound Not Sight
   Integrated/Causal Marketing
4. Trigger Meaning
5. Peer-suasion

> The innate ability of mobile devices to empower ordinary consumers in a way that could land them in the national spotlight is highly fulfilling.

Leveraging the Power of Peer Influence

Maslow's hierarchy of needs provides a useful model for engaging with consumers directly and persuading them by triggering meaning. Another strategy for reaching consumers is to leverage the power of their peer networks (a process we call *Peer-suasion*™).

Within a mobile environment, friends can persuade friends more effectively than any unwelcome and disruptive marketing messages from brands.

Friends also have the ability to sell and recommend content over a peer-to-peer mobile platform. Showing people examples of their peers who are happily doing something tends to convince them that they, too, will be happy doing the same thing.

People tend to follow and imitate the actions of others, both actively and passively. It is difficult for most people to "go against the flow." We use the actions of others to decide on proper behavior for ourselves—especially when we view those others as being similar to ourselves.

This has important implications for companies that target mobile users. If a company delivers a service or product that triggers meaning within a community of like-minded users with a common psychological need (e.g., creating an identity, a common goal of MySpace users), the company can often benefit from viral marketing. That's how MySpace quickly became so popular. The service began as an online forum for local bands to advertise. Word spread and teens began using it as a place to establish their identities. As the service grew into a powerful force, it began to attract college students and finally advertisers.

MySpace is a powerful example of how companies' products and services that triggered meaning can suddenly turn viral, without any marketing effort or expense from the company itself. The potential for viral marketing could be even greater in the mobile space, due to the pervasiveness of mobile phones.

The opportunities that the world of mobile brings to companies are almost boundless. Mobile technology and applications are still in their infancy. The promise of mobile commerce revenues ultimately exceeding online commerce revenues seems likely to be fulfilled. Companies that understand the psychological components of persuasion, and who succeed in creating meaning for customers through the experiences they deliver, stand a far greater chance of success in persuading customers to use their mobile products and services than those who rely on traditional marketing and advertising methods.

End Notes

[1] For example, a recent study from the PEW Research Center indicates that only 2% of users watch video or TV programs on mobile phone (Rainie 2007).

---

² The Customer Persuasion Process™ was developed by the author's company, Rule 13. The complete process consists of five steps, including assessing business rules; harnessing customers' insights into innovation; delivering an experience; triggering meaning; and leveraging Peer-suasion™ (peers persuading one another). This chapter focuses on the last two steps in the process, which are at the heart of persuasion.

About the Author

George LeBrun is the founder and CEO of Rule 13. Positioned as "Business Futurists for the Experience Economy," the firm focuses on helping companies assess and realign their business rules, Web 2.0 strategies, and innovation methodologies. George has also been a member of the senior management team of several high-profile internet companies. He has worked in the media and entertainment industry as a senior executive and in creative roles for 20 years. He is a member of the Writers Guild of America, holds a law degree, sits on the Advisory Board to the University of Texas School of Business, and is a judge for the 11th Annual Webby Awards.

Citations

Rainie, L. (2007). The New Digital Ecology: *The growth and impact of the internet (and related technologies)*. http://www.pewinternet.org/presentation_display.asp?r=86.

Jaokar, A. & Fish, T. (2006). Mobile Web 2.0: *The Innovator's Guide to Developing and Marketing Next Generation Wireless/Mobile Applications.* Futuretext.

Perspective 15

Mobile Persuasion Design Principles

Mirjana Spasojevic, Senior Principal Scientist, Nokia Research
Rachel Hinman, Design Strategist, Adaptive Path
Will Dzierson, Mobile Interface Designer, Google

The last decade has witnessed significant developments of mobile and ubiquitous devices, services and applications. Initial concepts and prototypes in the mobile domain have evolved into pilot deployments and finally, commercial endeavors. Some early ideas that have been put to the test, such as text messaging or payments using RFID cards, have reached success and broader adoption. Other technologies, such as invocation of services using barcodes, QR or Semacodes have enjoyed considerable success in some markets, but missed the mark in others (e.g., the failure of Cue Cat in the North American market).

In this chapter we discuss the mobile user experience, especially focusing on applications and services. What are the important elements of this unique experience? What makes certain mobile applications and services sticky? What strategies lead to broader adoption? What persuades and motivates people to use their mobile phones to access the internet?

The answers to such questions carry important implications for mobile persuasion. In comparison to building persuasive technologies on the computer, building such technologies on mobile devices is simultaneously both easier and more difficult. The limited resources of these devices make the presentation of complex information and interaction harder. But the very personal nature of mobile devices, the fact that we carry them with us everywhere we go (especially cell phones)—helps to offset these limitations, and to make these devices compelling platforms for persuasion.

Designing the Mobile User Experience

Past experiences and research (Roto 2006) suggest five themes and principles that are important to consider in designing mobile applications and services, at least when it comes to persuading people to use mobile devices as an access point to the internet:

Focus on the Unique Characteristics of Mobile

Some well-established lessons from prior research and commercial development suggest that accessing the internet using mobile phones is difficult. The obstacles include, among others, the difficulty of text input through phone keys, small screen size, network speed and latency, cost, and problems with navigation on sites that are not optimized for mobile devices. Yet, despite the challenges, people *are* accessing the internet via their mobile phones. The specific cases of access can be motivated by saving money (e.g., accessing Yellow Pages on the phone versus calling 411), maintaining privacy (e.g., accessing personal stock portfolios at work) or habits (e.g., ordering pizza online using a cell phone, which can be easier than calling in an order).

However, in PC-centric cultures, such as those in North America or Europe, persuading and motivating people to use their phones to access the internet often becomes a losing proposition when internet access is widely available in the home and at the office. In general, the value of the information and content accessed on the mobile phone must be uniquely suited for the situation and context, rather than being a directly downsized application or a website. Applications and services that uniquely combine content and that leverage the defining attributes of the mobile experience—such as QR codes—stand a better chance of communicating the value of the mobile internet experiences and motivating widespread use.

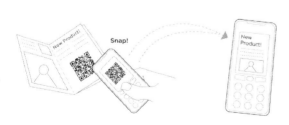

Figure 1 The inclusion of QR Code reading software on camera phones in Japan has led to a wide variety of new, consumer-oriented applications, aimed at relieving the user of the tedious task of entering data into their mobile phone. QR Codes storing addresses and URLS are becoming increasingly common in magazines and advertisements in Japan.

Think Always with You, not Just "on the Go"

People use their mobile phones to access the internet not only while on the go (in transit, in public venues, stores etc.), but also when they are not mobile (at home, in offices and schools, while visiting friends etc.). The context in which the internet can be accessed on the phone is as vast and variable as a day in one's life.

More powerful than the "on the go" metaphor is a common need of many users to always be in close physical proximity to their phones. Many people wake up to their mobile phone's alarm and feel intense anxiety when not within reach of the phone. The nature of an "always at hand" device that can provide information plays an important role in the decision of whether this device will be utilized to accomplish a task or satisfy a need. The unique relationship that people have with their mobile devices creates an enormous opportunity space for persuasion and motivation.

> Many mobile phone users experience intense anxiety if they are not in close proximity to their mobile phones. The unique relationship that people have with their mobile devices creates an enormous opportunity space for persuasion and motivation.

However, mobile applications and services also need to win over alternatives in a complex constellation of needs, motivation/urgency, physical environment, and alternatives, of which many could be fairly mundane and "low tech." A person searching for a piece of information, such as a restaurant name and phone number in order to make a dinner reservation, certainly has an option of utilizing search on a mobile device. But, depending on the person's physical context, he or she could as easily consult a physical phone book or newspaper or even call a friend in order to achieve the same result.

Build and Reinforce Common Ground and Identity

A great deal of research and anecdotal evidence suggests that people use mobile phones to make solo activities social. For example, while shopping for a piece of clothing, many have reported sending images to friends or family members to seek advice on a purchase. Many phone users describe text messaging as a remedy for loneliness and a quick and easy way to bring other people into their personal experience.

Figure 2 Mobile phones reinforce users' images of themselves—whom they think they are and aspire to be.

Mobile phones also act as signifiers to their owners, reinforcing whom they think they are and whom they aspire to be. This self-image is reflected both in the external appearance of their phones and in accessories, as well as choice of screen wallpapers and ringtones. Photos stored on the phone create a portable digital flipbook. They reflect both personal mementos and aspirations, reminders of what is important–motivating and inspiring people of their identity and dreams.

In addition, the phone is a vehicle for expressing accomplishment and sharing stories. Through storytelling, people are reinforcing existing relationships and shared understandings (Kindberg et al 2005). Their continued conversations build on the "common ground" and are not necessarily focused on accomplishments of a particular task with an identifiable beginning and end. The constant ping-pong of text messages that contain inside jokes or random photographs that only make sense to the people sharing them are often less about storytelling and more about reinforcing people's relationships with others. Few things are more important to people than their relationships to family, friends and colleagues. That's why the practices people have developed through their mobile devices that reinforce and build common ground are constant, ephemeral, and highly compelling.

Figure 3 MyAdhan has launched its prayer and fasting times SMS text message alert service to Muslims in the UK. After signing up on the MyAdhan website and configuring their accounts, users receive daily text messages on their cell phones related to prayer and fasting times specific to their locations.

Enable Access to What's Essential, Not Just Browsing

"Browsing" is a metaphor that has worked very well for the PC, but has not been as successful for accessing the internet via mobile phones. For many people, browsing the internet on a phone feels like looking at the world through a keyhole. Limited scale makes it difficult to see and interact with information. Borrowing the "browser" metaphor creates conceptual understanding, but also frequently sets up false expectations.

Certain new approaches have been developed to provide remedies, such as Nokia's Minimap browser, which allows users to see the whole page as a small thumbnail and then navigate through it quickly (Roto et al 2006). But the widespread adoption of these innovations requires the deployment of newer, more powerful phones. Rather than thinking about directly accessing internet sites developed for PC access, perhaps a better goal is to provide direct connections to the experiences that are essential to each user, such as weather forecasts and up to date news, and delivering them in a format that is designed for mobile phones.

Consider What Emerging Markets Can Teach Us about the Fundamentals of Mobility

Emerging markets, such as those in India, parts of Asia-Pacific and Africa have much to teach us about people's ability to adapt simple mobile technologies to coordinate fairly sophisticated actions and ad-hoc applications. While the generative need for these applications has been based largely on the lack of availability of 2G–2.5G network infrastructure in the developing world, the fundamental needs that these applications serve are telling. They are typically operated purely via SMS and center around activities as varied as group coordination for agricultural needs, public health alerts, voting on controversial issues, dating, and prayer time notification, among many other activities. One example is Voice SMS (via the Grameenphone in India).

> **Being mobile is less about technology than about culture, connectedness and fundamental human needs. Few human needs are more compelling than access to information and communication.**

Upon examining the needs that these simple technologies serve, it becomes clear that being mobile is much less about technology, and much more about culture, connectedness and fundamental human needs. Few human needs are more compelling than access to information and communication.

Conclusion

We believe that the design themes and principles outlined in this chapter, while in some aspects straightforward and obvious, provide a good recipe for building successful mobile applications and services. The natural tendency to miniaturize PC applications and move them to the latest version of the mini-computer platform must be balanced with the realistic expectations that these resource-poor devices can provide and the true nature of their role in people's lives.

Despite the nature of technical improvements, human attention remains one constant resource that cannot be divided toward too many different targets at any point in time. The true nature of successful mobile applications points to specific situations when they fill a human need in a unique way: they are sufficiently simple to learn and use, and the benefits are obvious to everyone.

About the Authors

Mirjana Spasojevic works at the newly opened Nokia Research Center in Palo Alto, California. In her role as a user research evangelist and a passionate advocate for very human mobile experiences, she focuses on ethnographic and lab-based studies of mobile technologies. In the last several years she has been investigating how and why people use camera phones and has been conducting international studies of mobile web services. Prior to Nokia, Mirjana has worked as a senior design researcher at Yahoo! Mobile business unit, and a senior research scientist and project manager at HP Labs where she was a member of the Cooltown program. She holds a Ph.D. in computer science from Penn State University.

Rachel Hinman is a design strategist for Adaptive Path. Her focus is on developing insights about people and using those insights to create valuable user experiences. Rachel's passion for people, design and business has been the driving force of her 10-year career in design. Rachel received her Masters Degree in design planning from the Institute of Design in Chicago in 2004. Prior to Adaptive Path, she worked within Yahoo!'s mobile group, employing user centered research and design methods to inform the design of Yahoo!'s mobile products. Her clients and previous employers have included IDEO, Microsoft, General Motors and Kaiser Permanente.

Will Dzierson is a mobile interface designer at Google. His focus is on designing highly usable mobile experiences that are grounded in a firm understanding of user needs, habits, motivations and context. Will began work in mobile six years ago designing and developing enterprise solutions for the mobile workforce and for higher education, including Harvard Medical School. He has since designed and developed mobile experiences for companies including Yahoo!, SoftBank/Yahoo! Japan, PepsiCo, Bose, Caterpillar, AholdUSA/Stop&Shop and the Smithsonian Institution. His current major areas of interest and design research center around mobile design solutions for emerging markets and the developing world and mobile group coordination and decision making.

Citations

Cue Cat http://cuecat.com/

MyAdhan http://www.myadhan.com/index.php?cid=Adverts-Textback&pid=1&tid=0

Kindberg, T., Spasojevic, M., Fleck, R., Sellen, A. (2005) I Saw This and Thought of You: Some Social Uses of Camera Phones. Proceeding of ACM CHI.

QR code http://en.wikipedia.org/wiki/QR_Code

Roto, V (2006) Web Browsing on Mobile Phones - Characteristics of User Experience. Doctoral dissertation, Helsinki University of Technology.

Roto, V., Popescu, A., Koivisto, A., Vartiainen, E. (2006) Minimap–a Web Page Visualization Method for Mobile Phones. Proceedings of ACM CHI.

Semacode http://en.wikipedia.org/wiki/Semacode

The Bigger Picture

Perspective 16

The Need for Simplicity

Martin Cooper, Executive Chair, ArrayComm, LLC

> *Editors' Note: Martin Cooper is the inventor of the portable cellular handset and the first person to make a call on a portable cell phone, which took place in April 1973, to the bewilderment of passers-by in a New York City street. He continues to advance technology, regulation and business practices in the wireless industry.*

It is inspiring and heartwarming to witness, in this book, the product of bright, fresh minds who are working on a problem that I started to think about before many of the authors were born. Personal mobile access to the world has the ability to make us more productive, safer and healthier; and to educate and entertain us. That has been a dream—and the mobile persuasion community is adding substance and fresh thinking to bring that dream to reality.

In this book, B.J. Fogg refers to the mobile phone as "the most important platform for motivating and persuading people." Of course, I agree with him, but calling this extraordinary tool a "mobile phone" is far too constraining. What has evolved over the past 34 years since commercialization of cellular telephony is a personal appliance that gives the individual instant and low-cost access to huge numbers of other individuals and to even greater sources of content. To some people, this appliance may be a mobile phone, but it will certainly evolve over time into a broad spectrum of devices that are tailored to the needs of the individuals who carry them and that are optimized to satisfy these needs.

If I may paraphrase B.J. Fogg's three fundamental attributes of this new platform for motivating and persuading people:

- love: people carry their mobile phones because they want to, not because they're forced to
- presence: the appliance is there when you need it

- instant access: to a world of content

to which I would add one more key attribute:

- simplicity

People love their mobile phones, and carry them wherever they go. B.J. and other authors want us to avail ourselves of this ubiquity by adding more functionality to the phones. This may be the only concept in this book with which I disagree. There are only two broad applications for mobile phones in the world today, voice communications and texting. At least for some people, mobile phones are optimized for these two functions. There are many other devices that attempt to perform other functions, such as email, web access, and music delivery. But I observe that when these additional functions are added, the utility of some of the other functions always becomes suboptimal. A smart phone that does email is usually a lousy voice device. Perhaps Apple will figure out how to make an optimal iPod combined with a mobile phone, but it will most certainly not be a device that is simple to use.

When a device or service purports to do all things for all people, it usually doesn't do any of them very well.

Certainly there will be persuasive techniques that can be achieved on a simple mobile phone and, in fact, in the early stages of mobile persuasive technology, these techniques will be prevalent. It would be a mistake, however, to attempt to foist on the public a suboptimal appliance—that is, an appliance that doesn't quite do the job right, or that is more complicated than it has to be, or that costs too much when an optimized appliance will do a better job. I don't have to remind you that, ultimately, it is the general public who will make the decision about whether they want to expose themselves to persuasion.

I cannot overemphasize the importance of simplicity as the basis for persuasive appliances and services. The wireless industry has already disenfranchised major segments of the public by creating mobile phones that are difficult to use and by adding features to phones that not only reduce their utility but make them useless for some people.

Jitterbug Phone: A Case Study in Simplicity

I offer a case study of the Jitterbug phone to illustrate the importance of simplicity in a device and the necessity to build, not only an appliance, but also a complete infrastructure that supports both utility and simplicity. The target market for the Jitterbug is people who are intimidated by complexity. While these people tend to be older, there are many young people who find existing mobile phones overly complicated and burdened with features that are useless to them.

The Jitterbug phone, as shown on the right in Figure 1, has big buttons and big numbers that can be seen without wearing glasses. The phone fits comfortably in the palm of a hand. There are no multiple function buttons or submenus; each button does exactly what it says and nothing more. There are no "bars" to inform you about "signal strength." Presence of dial tone (remember that?) informs you that there is an adequate signal. There are no buttons on the outside surface that can be accidentally depressed. There is a rubber ear piece that locates the phone precisely on the ear and that helps reject outside noise.

Figure 1 Both designs for the Jitterbug phone have large buttons and make the functions clear.

The Jitterbug has no camera, MP3 player, or web browser. It does have voice recognition, a mailbox, the ability to display photographs sent from the Web, and other features, but none of these features appear unless the user wants them.

More important than the physical structure of the phone is the simplicity inherent in the supporting infrastructure. When the user depresses the "0" or the "OPERATOR" button, an operator answers the user by name and is aware of the user's profile. The operator can complete a call when asked to "get my son," or "get my doctor." The operator can also update the user's phone book or add and delete features. The latter can also be done at a website by the user or the user's family.

While the Jitterbug phone and service are extremely simple, the supporting infrastructure for the phone is complex. There are 11 companies whose services are woven together by GreatCall, Inc., which offers Jitterbug.

I hope that the point of this case study is clear: The products and services that are the basis of a "simple" offering can be exceedingly complex, and the process for creating these products and services can be even more so. But the rewards of producing a "simple" mobile product and service are potentially great. Consider that the Jitterbug, introduced in November of 2006, had tens of thousands of subscribers by April of 2007, and growth is accelerating.

The Future of Mobile Persuasion

Some of the applications described in this book can be achieved with existing mobile phones. Most will do better if their platform is optimized for the specific application. But will cellular operators agree to allow a variety of new devices to operate on their networks? The answer, today, is "probably not." But the cellular world is changing in ways that support the concept of mobile persuasion. New technology is on the horizon that will increase competition and lower cost. An example of this is the WiMAX platform. WiMAX is a new mobile standard that will provide data speeds in excess of a megabit per second at costs far lower than existing mobile services. The advent of WiMAX will drive existing carriers to adopt new technology and new practices to the benefit of the innovators characterized in this book and to the general public.

The elderly today, absent the Jitterbug, often have great difficulty in using mobile phones. Their children, the "baby boomers," have adopted mobile phones but use them mostly for voice communications. Their grandchildren are taking pictures, playing music and conducting their business affairs with handheld devices. And their great-grandchildren will be unaware of the concept of a wired phone. It is the latter for whom the concept of mobile persuasion will be a reality. Thirty-four years after the introduction of the mobile phone, the wireless industry is starting to get it right. I know the mobile persuasion community will do even better.

About the Author

Martin Cooper is executive chairman and founder of ARRAYCOMM, Inc., and chairman of GreatCall, Inc. He is widely recognized as a pioneer in the personal communications industry and as an innovator in spectrum management. He is an inventor who introduced, in 1973, the first portable cellular radiotelephone and has been called the father of portable cellular telephony. Martin spent 29 years at Motorola as a vice president, division manager and corporate R&D director. Martin is a graduate of the Illinois Institute of Technology from where he received Bachelor's (1950) and Master's (1956) degrees in electrical engineering and an honorary Ph.D. (2004). He serves on the Illinois Institute of Technology's Board of Trustees.

Perspective 17

The Jetson Kids Reboot HealthCare

Susan Ayers Walker
Michael Sarfatti
Founders, SmartSilvers Alliance

In the immediate future the largest market for mobile persuasion may not be kids or college students but Baby Boomers. As shown in this book and elsewhere, the wave of mobile health products is growing. We believe Boomers are ideally positioned to ride this new wave into the future.

Born between 1946 and 1964, Baby Boomers (which includes ourselves) are a generation that loves technology. We were influenced by the futuristic world of the Jetsons®, living an imaginary life with flying cars, household robots, and ubiquitous communication networks. We grew up watching the  crew of the Starship Enterprise, wondering if the wireless "Beam me up Scotty" device could be designed in our lifetime. As we grew older, our generation invented disruptive technologies such as the internet, personal computers, the Mac and Windows operating systems, AOL, and the World Wide Web. So it seems clear that we'll continue innovating and adopting new technology. And this includes mobile health innovations.

Boomers and Mobile Health

We believe that Boomers won't be satisfied with "growing old gracefully." Rather, we will turn to mobile technology to improve our health and increase our social connectedness. As chronic conditions arise, we will want the ability to self-monitor our health, educate ourselves, motivate active lifestyles, and get advice from trusted medical sources.

We may not be able to dissolve and teleport our bodies from one location to another in our lifetime, but by using non-invasive, wearable and proximity body sensor systems, such as the VivoMetrics LifeShirt® and BodyMedia® SenseWear, we will be able to continuously monitor, record, and analyze our personal health conditions. With such technology, we would have the capability to transmit results from trusted, do-it-yourself screening tests for chronic conditions ranging from high cholesterol to blood-borne infections into a healthcare network that would analyze the data and raise a red flag alert to triage nursing if a declining trend was suspected.

The health phone

We believe the mobile phone will become a primary channel for delivering better health to Boomers. This includes applications to support smoking cessation, access to health records, food intake monitoring, blood glucose monitoring, and cardiac and vital-signs monitoring. The health phone platform will empower health and wellness by providing personal coaching and a "social network" connecting users to healthcare experts and emergency networks as well as to mental health and caregiving advice. Devices will help aging Boomers manage exercise and wellness through the use of personal trainer technology that takes blood pressure readings and encourages more exercise and diet modification. Such systems, which are installed in the home and connect to mobile devices are already being offered by Health Hero Network®, Elite Care®, Honeywell HomMed®, Philips Motiva, and BeWell Mobile.

Hello. . . texting your pill bottle

In addition to adopting wearable technology and mobile health applications, Boomers are a growing market for specialized mobile health devices. Consider SIMpill, an application designed for people who need to take medication on a regular basis. Here's how it works: The SIMpill container cap has a transmission device. When the smart pill bottle is opened, it sends a SMS text message to a central server. The message contains the pill bottle ID, a time stamp and information about the battery status of the pill bottle. When the server receives the SMS, it checks the schedule set-up for the pill bottle to be sending the message. If no message is received within the schedule's tolerances, the server produces a number of responses—e.g., sending a text message reminder to the patient's handset, sending a text message prompt to a family member or caregiver, prompting them to visit the patient to assess the cause of non-compliance. Data on levels of compliance as measured by the device are stored for future analysis and use.

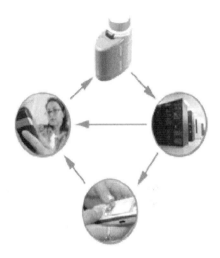

The Potential for Mobile Health

Besides SIMPill, many other health-focused technologies are now available or in development . These innovations will create a foundation for mobile persuasion. Note how the following near-term applications are well-suited to address the health issues facing Boomers.

Health and wellness management

By using a Bluetooth-enabled device such as a blood pressure monitor, weight scale, or cholesterol monitor, the user will be able to collect health data that is wirelessly transmitted to other Bluetooth devices, such as a mobile phone, PDA, or health appliance. The data also could be sent to the patient's caregiver for remote monitoring and health management.

Chronic disease management

Using a Bluetooth sensor, chronically ill patients will be able to measure their vital health indicators on their own or with their caregiver via a Bluetooth computation engine such as a PDA, PC, or mobile phone.

Fitness and workout tracking

Users will be able to monitor their success in achieving fitness goals by tracking health data during a workout with a Bluetooth sensor, such as a calorie counter, weight scale, or heart rate monitor. Data will be wirelessly transmitted to a Bluetooth computation engine on a PDA, PC, mobile phone, etc. allowing the user to track his or her progress relative to their fitness goals.

Remote biosensor measurement

With a Bluetooth medical kit connected to a set-top box or PC, patients could have their health status checked from the comfort of their own home by conducting a phone or video visit with their caregiver. Once the information is gathered, it would be transmitted to the caregiver in order for the patient's health to be monitored.

Making Mobile Health a Reality

There are still many issues to overcome before we will see mobile health become a widespread reality in the marketplace. From a user's perspective, the biggest challenge is simplicity. Unfortunately, the overall trend in consumer electronics is to add more features and greater complexity. We believe that simplicity is vital for widespread adoption of health innovations. Related to simplicity is the issue of size. While smaller devices are nicely portable, at some point the tiny buttons and screens create frustration, especially for people with diminished eyesight.

Designing a usable device is vital, but the most challenging issue of all centers on the system of healthcare delivery. Medical device companies have large hurdles to overcome as they attempt to introduce consumer health devices into overly complex, isolated healthcare systems that lack clear incentives to adopt new technologies. We believe the healthcare system is shortsighted. The faster healthcare organizations can understand the value and savings that mobile health provides, the faster these innovations will make a real difference in health. We need a convincing demonstration that these new technologies will minimize the need for costly hospital visits and enable early detection of potential health problems and a reduction in expensive treatments.

In the future, aging consumers will proactively manage their own health, empowering themselves to address chronic, age-related disabilities head on. The pervasiveness of mobile phones and portable devices, combined with security features and Bluetooth technology, will contribute to the interoperability of home care and chronic medical devices. This will result in a better quality of life for the individual while reducing the overall cost of their healthcare. Hopefully this new technology will arrive just in time for the Boomer generation to know that their innovations became a reality and they can enjoy the second half of their lives living like the Jetsons.

End Notes

Continua Health Alliance® http://www.continuaalliance.org/

Bluetooth® SIG, Inc. http://www.bluetooth.com/Bluetooth/SIG/

USB Implementers Forum, Inc. http://www.usb.org/home

Images

"Future Convergence" – copyright (c) Michael Sarfatti, SmartSilvers Alliance. All rights reserved (http://www.smartsilvers.com)

VivoMetrics LifeShirt® System, Copyright(c) VivoMetrics, Inc. All rights reserved. (http://www.vivometrics.com)

SIMpill Medication Dispenser, Copyright(c) SIMpill (Pty.) Ltd. All rights reserved. (http://www.simpilldirect.com/)

About the Authors

Susan Walker has over 40 years experience in emerging technologies; encompassing semiconductors, hardware/software design, and applications development. Susan cofounded the SmartSilvers Alliance with the goal to "leverage technologies that foster active aging" ™. The mission is to promote deployment of innovative, consumer-friendly products and services that cater to our aging society, supporting independence, mobility, and quality of life. Susan is on the global board of the MIT Enterprise Forum, which supports entrepreneurial innovation. Susan holds a BSEE from Northeastern University and an MSCS from Rutgers. As a journalist, she is the computer and technology writer for AARP.

Michael Sarfatti, cofounder of the SmartSilvers Alliance, has over 30 years experience in a variety of industries, including petrochemical, financial services, and information technology, holding positions in engineering, training, marketing/sales, business development and executive management. Since 1988, he has been an officer and director of the MIT Club of Northern California. Michael was also the cofounder of the MIT Enterprise Forum of the Bay Area (dba MIT/Stanford Venture Lab, aka VLAB), currently serving on the organization's advisory board. Michael is a graduate of the Massachusetts Institute of Technology, earning Bachelors and Masters degrees in mechanical engineering, and is a registered professional mechanical engineer.

Perspective 18

Ethical Dangers of Mobile Persuasion

Jerry Michalski, President, Sociate

Mobile persuasion heralds a world alive with useful information about the immediate environment, as well as about your actions and reactions. Applications could range from just-in-time information about nearby objects of desire—ah! that gadget I've been coveting is on sale at this store to my right—to my favorite brainstorming scenario: An opt-in service that automatically rings your AA buddy if it notices you've been within 25 feet of a known bar for more than ten minutes.

I'm concerned about the dark side though. I'm worried that the capabilities already at hand and coming in the foreseeable future may open a Pandora's Box of opportunities to intrude and manipulate people. I'm worried that the developers of persuasive technologies have no "adult supervision" or ethical guidance on these matters. I'm worried that sometimes it's difficult to tell legitimate persuasion from coercion. And I'm worried that the people building these technologies have little understanding of the implications of what they're creating, and little recourse to call a halt when they do spot something amiss.

Despite all those concerns, I believe that with care, together we can create a field full of terrific, helpful, profitable services and applications, avoiding the coercive scenarios that might tempt some. But first, indulge me with a dive into the dark side of persuasion.

Never More Intimate

We have adopted intimate technologies before. Many of us wear watches, glasses, or contact lenses. Watches hug our wrists, helping us get to places on time. Contacts hug our eyes, helping us perceive the outside world. None of those technologies makes any of that intimate information available to others: Your watch doesn't send information about what you're writing; your lenses don't report back everything you see.

Now, we love our mobile phones. We keep them by our side all the time. Mine is my morning alarm clock and occasional handy camera. Other people use theirs as watches, music jukeboxes, email hubs, calculators, flashlights, universal remote controls, social networking tools, research and navigation aids, movie makers and more. In some countries, mobile phones are easy to use to pay for things. It's hard to imagine we once went out in the evening and managed to meet people and have fun without mobile phones.

Alas, mobile phones do report all sorts of information about your activities. And the technologies of mobile persuasion—mobile phones, wireless networks, text messages, location coordinates—together create an environment of unprecedented intimacy, much of which is accessible to others.

What you browse on the net, whom you call, where you are during the day: All of this information can be tracked and stored in databases. A surprising amount of the information is easily accessible, because the financial incentives for making it accessible are strong.

Oh, There You Are!

Mobile carriers expect to make extra revenues with your location data. Governments have mandated that mobile phones be locatable, because too many people were calling in with emergencies with no idea of where they were. Carriers might sell this location information to third parties, who will use it to drop location-specific advertisements, coupons, or other enticements in front of us, without our permission.

As mobile phones become primary transaction tools and become even more useful, the thoroughness with which they will "see" what we do and with whom we do it is staggering. Never before have we had a populace that might be so easily and thoroughly surveilled.

I'm equally concerned about both governmental Big Brother scenarios and corporate invasions of privacy.

Who's Minding the Store?

One reason to be extremely wary is that nobody seems to be minding the store while all this new mobile technology is developed and deployed. We do have privacy laws, as well as laws against fraud, theft, and more. But laws have become oddly extensible and malleable through software, as Lawrence Lessig has noted.

The 1998 Digital Millennium Copyright Act (DMCA), passed to protect copyrighted works from being replicated without permission, has an anti-circumvention provision that makes it a felony to try to get around the protections. As a result, a software engineer writing code for a music player on your mobile phone is, in effect, creating new laws. If you break them, you've committed a federal crime. This aspect of the DMCA already has had an adverse effect on fair use.

We don't know what path this story will take. The important point is that nobody is watching over this field. Biotech scientists have bioethics committees and medical ethics experts. Financial engineers have the SEC or similar bodies watching. Who watches the mobile phone application coders? Those coding web-based services? Who knows today that it matters?

What's worse, the people doing the coding (and planning what to code) have neither guidelines for identifying when they might be treading in dicey mobile-persuasion territory, nor the means to call a halt to the dicey operation, the way an assembly-line worker might pull a cord to halt the assembly line when something is going wrong.

When Does Persuasion = Manipulation?

To make matters more complex, one person's manipulation may be another's idea of great service.

Some applications we will pretty uniformly agree on as egregious. Many others will be clearly useful and ethical. Between those extremes lies a large gray area, an area few people are exploring (Rushkoff 1999), and nobody is really mapping yet.

As an example of a manipulative service, imagine a web-based shopping service you access through your mobile phone that does deep clickstream analysis. The service data-mines and tests where you go and what you do. In the process, it discovers that you tend to click on orange-colored ads more often than others (or ads featuring scantily-clad women; you choose the variable). So they change the ads for things they want to sell you to orange— and maybe even custom-color your cigarettes orange.

Some Solutions

There are many ways we might increase the consideration of ethics in the design of mobile persuasion systems, including disclosure, technological markers, industry associations, labeling, watchdogs, privacy laws and movements, bypassing cellular phone companies, and education and mindfulness. I consider a few of these below.

Voluntary Disclosure

Voluntary disclosure works—sort of. For example, movie ratings are a voluntary system, created by the movie industry to prevent formal regulations from being enacted.

One of the drawbacks of disclosure for persuasive technologies is that the persuaders may be loath to disclose the secret methods they have developed. This is completely understandable. These trade secrets may well be essential to their advantage over competitive offers.

One hope I have that voluntary disclosure will grow is that we're entering an era in which companies want to win the real loyalty of customers. To get true loyalty, companies will have to be more authentic, to connect with customers in meaningful ways.

So my hope is that disclosures will become a competitive advantage. They will be a major way that companies can show what they're busy doing behind the curtain. The *quid pro quo* for divulging such secrets is greater trust from the people subjected to those methods, especially when the disclosures show that manipulative options weren't used to win their loyalty.

> My hope is that disclosures will become a competitive advantage. They will be a major way that companies can show what they're busy doing behind the curtain.

Watchdogs

If voluntary disclosure is only partially useful, it may be made more useful if infractions are vigorously pursued. That is, if some organization(s) actively brings bad publicity to those that deserve it, behaving well will be a more profitable strategy.

In other domains, watchdog groups have had great effects, though in most cases the transgressions being watched still occur. More recently, the Sunlight Foundation is bringing data into public view in order to reduce corruption in the U.S. Congress.

Bypass

One of the principal threats to our privacy and behavioral peace is the industry most likely to provide the services platform that mobile persuaders will use: the cellular phone companies. The cellular carriers see clearly the profit potential of our locational and behavioral data.

One answer to this threat is bypass: wresting independence from the cellular carriers by using alternative data transports, such as the metropolitan Wi-Fi systems springing up around the world, or the loosely knit open Wi-Fi networks such as FON.

Education and Mindfulness

Finally, raising awareness can help to mitigate unethical behaviors, but decades of consumer education about the wily ways that some advertisers (and some politicians) use have left us only marginally more literate citizens. Irony and cynicism abound, but the techniques of manipulation work almost as well as ever.

Nevertheless, greater awareness of the issues and a heightened ability to distinguish ethical from unethical applications of mobile persuasion will give people more ability to pull that brake handle. Greater mindfulness may be one of the most potent tools against those who would use the power of persuasion in unethical ways.

> Greater mindfulness may be one of the most potent tools against those who would use the power of persuasion in unethical ways.

Despite my rather gloomy forecast, I'd like to close with two more positive thoughts. First, it's easy to do something constructive to encourage the ethical use of mobile persuasion. I'm starting a nonprofit organization that will use both negative and positive reinforcement: It will "out" the most egregious persuaders as it persuades the other persuaders that they ought voluntarily to use better methods.

My final thought is a restatement of the positive note I struck at the start. There is marvelous potential for good in the technologies of mobile persuasion. People will be able to find what they need, meet people they like, change behaviors they don't like, and much more. If we build these systems mindfully and openly, the field of mobile persuasion will be greeted warmly. It's our collective responsibility to build ethics into our processes and offers as we design this intimate future.

About the Author

Jerry Michalski is a guide to the relationship economy: He helps organizations nurture authentic relationships with their natural audiences or customer bases, as well as among their employees. This process builds lasting loyalty with customers, increases margins, and increases cooperation among employees; boosting collaboration, innovation, and execution. Jerry is a pattern finder, lateral thinker, Gladwellian connector, and explorer of the interactions between technology, society, and business. He is also a humanist—a champion for people in the face of technology. In this latter role, he is forming a center to address aspects of ethics in the creation of technologies.

Citations

Rushkoff, D. (1999). *Coercion: Why We Listen to What "They" Say.* Riverhead.

Redefining Persuasion for a Mobile World

Dean Eckles, Mobile Research Specialist, Persuasive Technology Lab, Stanford University

During World War II, social scientists began to conduct experiments on wartime propaganda, such as leaflets dropped from the sky, voice broadcasts via radio, and indoctrination films (Hovland et. al. 1949). The study of persuasion in social science thus was born, and persuasive messages became the atoms of this new science. Since then, most researchers have defined persuasion as successfully changing people's attitudes or opinions by using messages (O'Keefe 2002, Wood 2003).

Interactive persuasive technology does not fit this mold. In 1998, when laying the foundation for captology[1], B.J. Fogg changed the definition of persuasion in two ways. First, in this new definition, persuasion can be embodied in a variety of experiences, not just symbolic messages. Second, Fogg proposed that persuasion should be defined by the *intention* to persuade, whether or not the effort succeeds.

I propose that mobile technology requires yet another shift in our definition of persuasion. This change has two parts. First, mobile persuasive technology continues to make messages less useful as the atoms of persuasion. Second, the way in which people adopt mobile technology into their lives reshapes what it means to accept and internalize persuasion.

Mobile persuasive technology can be usefully seen as creating what I call *persuasive faculties*—new senses and reasoning abilities that are designed to change attitudes and behaviors. That is, when people adopt mobile technologies, *these technologies can persuade by becoming part of how people interact with the world.* This new perspective evokes ideas of trans-humanism and cyborgs, but it also has real value for studying and designing mobile persuasive technologies that people deeply integrate into their lives.

In this chapter, I outline this shift in the definition of persuasion and describe how it changes the outlook on influence and persuasive technology. But first, something concrete—an example that illustrates how this perspective can play out in mobile persuasive technology.

> Mobile persuasive technology creates persuasive faculties—new senses and reasoning abilities that are designed to change attitudes and behaviors. That is, when people adopt mobile technologies, these technologies can persuade by becoming part of how people interact with the world.

Example

As Neil walks to a local market, his mobile device provides information and media, using his glasses to annotate the world around him. When he sees a flower shop, he also sees a note on the shop asking whether there's anyone he'd like to buy flowers for and providing some suggestions. When he reaches the market, his best friend's favorite potato chips are basking in a warm digital glow. Every day, all day, Neil's mobile technology shapes how he perceives the world. Even when his technology adds nothing to his perception, this too has meaning. For example, if the potato chips aren't glowing, Neil knows that none of his friends has evaluated them.

The Persuasive Message

Persuasive messages fit into genres: a magazine ad, a speech at a rally, propaganda leaflets dropped from a plane, or a television spot.[2] These genres can help consumers know when they are being persuaded. Persuaders also draw on patterns of the genre in creating their messages.

Fogg (2002, 2007) pointed out that with persuasive technology, often the genre boundaries disappear because the experiences are too new and the technology is so flexible that the digital experience can defy categorization. A few message genres have emerged, such as banner ads, search advertising, and demo nag messages. However, I believe that interactive persuasive technology will not be categorized by genres of messages to the same extent as previous media.

Instead of message genres, new genres of *persuasive procedures and processes* are emerging in interactive technology. This is most clearly exemplified by persuasive games and simulations (Bogost 2007 and in this volume), and also by installation and sign-up wizards.[3] Unlike the designers of persuasive messages, the designers of these technologies are creating interactive experiences whose persuasive power comes from a series of interactions, not from a set of static messages.

> Unlike the designers of persuasive messages, the designers of persuasive technologies are creating interactive experiences whose persuasive power comes from a series of interactions, not from a set of static messages.

In mobile persuasive technology, messages are no longer the atoms of persuasion. Even though text messaging (SMS) is currently a dominant means for mobile persuasion (e.g. Levine, this volume), these messages do not exist in isolation. They are most effective when presented as part of an ongoing interaction.

For example, Perspective 12 (Holmen) describes a successful mobile marketing campaign—an ongoing text messaging service that warns opt-in customers that gas prices will increase in a few hours. In this context, the messages at the appropriate times, and the lack of messages at other times, serve as a fulfillment of a promise to customers rather than static atoms of persuasion.

> In the future, mobile technology will persuade us by controlling what we perceive and what actions we can take in that particular moment.

Persuasive technology based on other mobile platforms will amplify this trend. The lone message will become less important, replaced by contextual information that comes to people based on their goals, their location, their activity, and—possibly—their state of mind. In other words, in the future mobile technology will persuade us by controlling what we perceive and what actions we can take in that particular moment. This future is illustrated in Neil's potato chip experience above.

	Early social science (Hovland et. al. 1949, Wood 2003)	Persuasive technology (Fogg 1998, 2002, 2003)	Mobile persuasive technology
Unit of design and analysis	symbolic message	diverse experiences (tools media, social actors)	persuasive faculties (analogous to new senses and reasoning capabilities)
Success	internalization of the message	behavior (or attitude) change	adoption as internalization
Defined by	success	intention	intention

Table 1. Basic differences among three perspectives on persuasion.

Internalizing the Change

While the meaning of persuasion will change—becoming an ongoing, contextual process that is mediated by our mobile technology—what it means for persuasion to succeed will also change. In the classic social science view, persuasion is successful by definition and only succeeds through internalization of the persuasive message; internalization means embracing a new attitude or opinion that continues even when the influencer is not around or when someone else tries to change the attitude again. In the new world of mobile persuasion, this classic type of internalization may often be eclipsed by another type: deep adoption as internalization.

Adoption of mobile persuasive technology is a new form of internalization. When someone adopts a mobile persuasive technology, deeply integrating it into his or her life and depending on it as credible, this is an extreme form internalization. Rather than internalizing a fixed set of attitudes by being subjected to a persuasive message, this adoption internalizes a new process for acquiring and reinforcing attitudes as part of a larger, accepted program. For example, when people use a mobile personal coach that monitors their actions and surroundings and provides constant feedback, the coach becomes a new way of learning about the world: it is internalized as a persuasive means for acquiring attitudes. It becomes the guide for perceiving the world and for taking action.

Persuasive Faculties

The previous two sections have explained reasons for developing a new perspective on persuasion as mobile persuasion becomes common. The new perspective proposes that

- messages are not the basic units of analysis of persuasion, and

- deeply integrated technology is the new form of internalization.

How does this new form of persuasion play out in the real world? I will explain by introducing the concept of persuasive faculties.

Persuasive faculties are technologically mediated ways of perceiving, reasoning about, and interacting with the world that are designed to bring about attitude and behavior change. When people adopt mobile persuasive technology, they can gain a new persuasive faculty.

Some persuasive faculties are like new senses. Just as some devices allow people to see infrared light, persuasive faculties will allow people to perceive new aspects of the world. From a persuasion standpoint, the key insight is this: When senses are created by adopting technology, they can be designed persuasively. For example, a faculty that enables sensing air quality can be designed to change attitudes and behaviors (see Perspective 10 by Consolvo, Paulos, and Smith). Likewise, Neil (the potato chip example) "sees" his friends' opinions in a way that changes how he reacts to new products and experiences. Persuasive senses generally follow a push model: The sense augments or interrupts in response to the world.

Some persuasive faculties are like new reasoning capabilities. Like being able to do quick mental math, new reasoning capabilities allow people to make calculations or retrieve information. These capabilities can be built for persuasion, whether they take the form of simulations or searches. For example, being able to simulate the results of different social or conversational choices could be persuasive. Persuasive reasoning capabilities are generally pull oriented: The person initiates using the capability when making decisions or trying to understand something.

This perspective reshapes how we conceive of persons in persuasion. The psychology of persuasion and even captology has viewed people as separate from technology; we are not part human and part machine. But this notion is likely to change. Fogg proposed that users have intimate relationships with their mobile devices, writing that "people don't adopt mobile devices; they marry them" (Fogg 2002, p. 192). But this still leaves the technology *outside* of the person. I propose here that humans will welcome digital augmentations that empower them. But even as people gain new faculties, they will also be subject to persuasion in new ways.

As noted earlier in this chapter, when we think about mobile technologies as creating persuasive faculties, it does conjure up the image of the cyborg—the trans-human, technologically augmented person.[4] In the persuasive faculty perspective, the technology is part of how the person interacts with the world. It creates new opportunities for features of the world to directly generate reasons for and against beliefs and choices. We might even say that the technology creates new cognitive biases and heuristics by design.

> I propose that humans will welcome digital augmentations that empower them. But even as people gain new faculties, they will also be subject to persuasion in new ways.

This new view of persuasion is on the cutting edge: The need to make this shift won't happen overnight, and the new view won't account for all cases and ends. In many situations, the new definition of persuasion will live in harmony with previous interpretations of what it means to change attitudes, behaviors, or both.

The title of this book makes claims about the future of behavior change. I think this is accurate: Mobile persuasive technology is a key means by which attitude and behavior change will be carried out in the future. Because this is the coming reality, I believe we need to understand persuasion in a new way so we can better investigate the dynamics behind attitude and behavior change in the coming years.

End Notes

[1] Captology is the study of computers as persuasive technologies (Fogg, 1998).

[2] This is not to say that these messages are easily distinguishable by their recipients as persuasion. Rather, the point is that there is something symbolic that is the message that can be picked out and that is a useful object for analysis.

[3] These examples fall into the persuasive medium and tool roles of Fogg's functional triad (Fogg 2002). But the social actor role also includes persuasive procedures and processes. See Guéguen (2002) and Guéguen & Jacob (2001), which are studies of sequential request strategies in persuasive technology.

[4] Though it might be useful to think of people as cyborgs even not considering mobile devices (consider contact lenses, hearing aids, and even shoes), never before have such ever-present augmentations been so flexible or had such far-reaching consequences for persuasion and influence. For another perspective on cyborgs, see Haraway (1991).

About the Author

Dean Eckles is a researcher and designer focused on interactions with mobile devices and persuasive technology. He is currently a mobile research specialist at the Persuasive Technology Lab at Stanford University.

His recent work includes studying context-aware mobile media sharing and consumption, privacy considerations, and disclosure behavior. His current research in the Stanford Persuasive Technology Lab focuses on uniquely mobile opportunities for persuasion—specifically, changing location-disclosure behavior and leveraging location information to persuade.

Dean is completing a master's degree in the Symbolic Systems Program at Stanford University, studying interaction design, persuasive technology, and the psychology that informs both. He holds a B.S. in Symbolic Systems and a B.A. in Philosophy, both from Stanford University.

Citations

Bogost I. (2006). *Unit Operations: An Approach to Videogame Criticism.* Cambridge, MA: the MIT Press.

Fogg, B.J. (1998). Persuasive Computers: Perspectives and Research Directions. *Proceedings of ACM CHI 98 Conference on Human Factors in Computing Systems,* 225–232. New York: ACM Press.

Fogg, B.J. (2002). *Persuasive Technology: Using Computers to Change What We Think and Do.* San Francisco: Morgan Kaufmann.

Fogg, B.J. (2003). Motivating, influencing, and persuading users. In *The human-computer interaction handbook: fundamentals, evolving technologies and emerging applications.* Human Factors And Ergonomics. Lawrence Erlbaum Associates, Inc. (pp. 358–370).

Fogg, B.J. (2007). Personal correspondence.

Guéguen, N. (2002). Foot-in-the-door technique and computer-mediated communication. *Computers in Human Behavior,* 18(1), 11–15.

Guéguen, N., Jacob, C. (2001). Fund-Raising on the Web: The Effect of an Electronic Foot-in-the-Door on Donation. CyberPsychology & Behavior 4:6, 705.

Haraway, D. (1991). A Cyborg Manifesto: Science, Technology, and Socialist-Feminism in the Late Twentieth Century. In *Simians, Cyborgs, and Women: The Reinvention of Nature.* Free Association. (pp. 149–181).

Hovland, C.I., Lumsdaine, A.A., Sheffield, F.D. (1949). *Experiments on Mass Communication.* Studies in social psychology in World War II, Vol. 3. Princeton, NJ: Princeton University Press.

O'Keefe, D. (2002). *Persuasion: Theory & Research.* Thousand Oaks, CA: Sage Publications.

Wood, W. (2003). Attitude Change: Persuasion and Social Influence. *Annual Review of Psychology,* 51, 539–570.

Your Perspective on Mobile Persuasion

At this point you've read 19 different perspectives on mobile persuasion. Now it's your turn. Perspective #20 belongs to you. We invite you to visit www.MobilePersuasion.com and share your insights with us.

Your personal experience with mobile persuasion may influence only a handful of appreciative readers. On the other hand, what you say might resonate with thousands of people in a way that academic research cannot. Who knows?

Here's what we do know: The most important insights in mobile persuasion are yet to come. And it seems likely that some very insightful thinkers about mobile persuasion will eventually find and read this book. You may be one of them.

The format for sharing is flexible. You can tell your story, describe a service that you find persuasive, explain your research, or talk about the challenges you see in mobile persuasion. You can contribute your perspective in text, pictures, or video. On the next page you'll find some some sample questions to get you started.

We look forward to seeing what you'll share.

B.J. Fogg, Ph.D.
Dean Eckles
Editors

Persuasive Technology Lab
Stanford University

Add Your Perspectives at www.MobilePersuasion.com

Here are some questions to get you thinking:

1. What are today's best examples of mobile persuasion?

2. How will mobile persuasion change your everyday life?

3. Why is health such a prominent focus for mobile persuasion?

4. How will mobile persuasion change social activism?

5. What are the most dangerous uses of mobile persuasion?

6. What factors will cause people to accept or reject mobile persuasion?

7. When is using mobile persuasion not ethical?

8. Which influence strategies work best in mobile persuasion?

9. What are the best uses for mobile persuasive games?

10. What is the "killer app" for mobile persuasion?

Appendix

Appendix

Increasing Persuasion Through Mobility

B.J. Fogg, Persuasive Technology Lab, Stanford University

Editors' Note: Some of B.J. Fogg's earlier writings relate to the theme of this book, including Chapter 8 of Fogg's book, *Persuasive Technology*, published by Morgan Kaufmann in 2002. In this appendix we present a condensed version of that chapter.

When it comes to motivating and influencing people, mobile technologies have clear advantages over desktop computers. Mobility adds two powerful ingredients to the persuasion recipe: timing and context. The importance of these two factors should not be a surprise. When skilled human persuaders hope to influence others, they select the time and place carefully. This can make the difference between success and failure. I propose the same is true for interactive technologies designed to persuade: Intervening at the right time and the right place increases the chances of getting results.

As you read the following hypothetical example of "Study Buddy," think about how connectivity and mobility enhance the product's ability to motivate and persuade.

The Study Buddy

> *Someday in the future, a freshman named Pamela sits in a college library and removes an electronic device from her purse. It's just smaller than a deck of cards, easily carried around, and serves as Pamela's mobile phone, information portal, entertainment platform, and personal organizer. She takes this device almost everywhere and feels a bit lost without it. Because she's serious about school, Pamela runs an application on her device called "Study Buddy." Here's what the application does:*

As Pamela begins her evening study session, she launches the Study Buddy system and views the display. Study Buddy congratulates her for studying for the third time that day, meeting the goal she set at the beginning of the academic quarter. The device suggests that Pamela start her study session with a five-minute review of her biology vocabulary words, then read the two chapters assigned for tomorrow's sociology lecture.

As Pamela reviews biology, the Study Buddy screen shows a cluster of shapes, which represent her classmates who are currently studying. This motivates her to continue studying.

Later that evening, as Pamela wraps up her work, she's curious about her mentor, Jean, so she turns to Study Buddy for information. Jean also subscribes to the Study Buddy system and has invited Pamela into her "awareness group."[1] Pamela sees a symbol on the display that indicates Jean is currently in one of the campus libraries. Jean is a good role model; she's a senior who was recently admitted to a top graduate school. Being a study mentor means that Jean has agreed to let Pamela remotely view Jean's studying habits. Using Study Buddy, Jean can send simple sounds and tactile cues such as vibration patterns to Pamela, to encourage her to study.

Although the preceding example may never become an actual product, the scenario illustrates how the system's mobile and connected qualities boost the potential for persuasion. In my view, mobility and networking represent an emerging frontier for persuasive technology. When you pack a mobile persuasive technology with you, you pack a source of influence. At any time (ideally, at the appropriate time), the device can suggest, encourage, and reward; it can track your performance or lead you through a process; it can provide compelling factual evidence or insightful simulations.

The Kairos Factor

As a constant companion, mobile devices are in a unique position to persuade. This persistent presence is what I call the "kairos factor." Taken from ancient Greek rhetoric, *kairos* is the principle of presenting your message at the opportune moment. Mobile technology makes it easy to intervene at the opportune moment for persuasion, as the technology can travel with users wherever they go.

By knowing a user's goals, routine, current location, and current task, mobile systems of the future will be able to determine when the user would be most open to persuasion in the form of a reminder, suggestion, or simulated experience. It may sense when the user has a need and step in to provide a solution.

For example, imagine how eBay.com might develop its recommendation engine to such a degree that as you lingered in a museum to admire sculptures by Auguste Rodin, the site could identify your interest in this artist and send you a special offer to buy prints of Rodin's work, if you have opted to receive such information.

The Importance of Application Design

In my research lab at Stanford University, we've debated how people view their mobile devices. Are they simply a tool? Are they like a faithful companion? Or do owners view their mobile devices as appendages, as part of themselves?

If indeed people view their mobile phones as extensions of themselves—as an integral part of who they are and what they can do—those who create persuasion experiences for mobile devices need to take particular care. The experiences likely to be appreciated are those that help people accomplish their *own* goals. Experiences that work against a person's goals or intrude into their lives may be viewed as a betrayal. Your device sold you out.

As I see it, people don't adopt mobile devices; they *marry* them. Some people spend more time with these devices than with any person in their lives, including their spouses. Because of this fact, designers need to design mobile interactions that will weather well, like a longstanding, comfortable friendship. The user experience should support an intensive, positive relationship between the user and the mobile application. Otherwise, the relationship is likely to be ended, like a bad marriage.

Persuasion through Connected Technology

Not all mobile devices are connected to a network. Those that are connected gain potential power to influence users because the devices can provide better information and can leverage social influence strategies. I address each topic in turn below.

Leveraging Current and Contingent Information

Connected devices are able to gather and report the most current, and therefore the most persuasive, information. For example, when eBay customers have the latest information delivered to them about their auction, this changes the eBay customer's experience. With this current information, bidders are invited back to the virtual auction and prompted to respond to being outbid. The currency of the information seduces people back into the eBay world, even when they're away from their Web browsers.

Connected products also are more persuasive because they can provide contingent information—that is, information that takes into account variables that are relevant to users, their goals, and their contexts. Think of a product designed to promote smart commuting. It could account for immediate personal needs ("I've got to get to work by 9 a.m. today, and I don't need to run errands during lunch"), enduring preferences ("I like the idea of taking public transportation"), passing constraints ("This morning I have only four dollars to spend"), and environmental variables (the weather and the traffic conditions). With these variables taken into account, the connected product can be more persuasive in proposing what commute option would be best for that day.

Persuasion through Social Influence

When mobile devices are connected to a network, they also gain the ability to use social influence to change people's attitudes and behavior. The study of social influence includes many theories and perspectives. In this condensed chapter, I'll touch only on two theories: social facilitation and social comparison.

Persuading through Social Facilitation

When I'm training for a big swim meet, I join a master's swim club and train as part of a team. I can work out fine alone, but when I'm swimming with a team, I find that my workouts are much better and I progress faster. I'm not alone. Since the late 1800s, sport psychologists have observed this same phenomenon: Most people exercise more effectively when they are with other people.[2]

The principle of social facilitation suggests that people perform better—more, longer, harder—when other people are present, participating, or observing.[3] Connected products can leverage this principle by creating new opportunities to generate social facilitation effects.

Because connected products can allow other people to be virtually present, the products can be used to motivate better performance by creating a virtual social group.[4] If a person is performing a well-learned activity—such as running on a treadmill—he or she will likely perform better if a connected product shows that other people are virtually present, performing the same activity.[5] You could even envision a completely virtual fitness facility: You work out at home but through connected technology you can see others doing the same thing, and you know they can see you.[6] This virtual presence would likely produce some of the same beneficial social facilitation effects of working out at a regular gym. This approach might also be used to inspire better performance from workers in remote locations, motivate students as they prepare for college entrance exams, or encourage higher bidding in online auctions.

To generate social facilitation effects, the representation of others doesn't need to be realistic at all.[7] Simple avatars could represent other people. Abstract shapes would probably work in some cases, as I described earlier in the Study Buddy scenario at the start of this chapter. Even bar graphs might effectively represent the presence and performance of others.

The Power of Social Comparison

The second social influence principle I'll address is social comparison. According to social comparison theory,[8] people seek information about others to determine how they compare and what they should be thinking or doing. In essence, we use people as a comparison point or a reality check.

The Study Buddy application at the start of this chapter uses social comparison as one of its strategies to promote better study habits. The connected device lets the student know when her classmates are studying. The point of this information isn't to put peer pressure on the user; instead, it's providing information about similar others—information that helps shape decisions and behaviors.

The social comparison effect is strengthened when it allows people to compare themselves to those who are similar to themselves in terms of age, ability, ethnicity, or another key attribute.[9]

Persuading through Intrinsic Motivation

In addition to extending the power of social influence principles, connected products can leverage the power of intrinsic motivation, a type of energizing force that arises directly from an activity or situation. Certain activities—playing the guitar, writing poetry, swimming at the beach—are inherently rewarding. Many people don't need external pressure or rewards to do these things; the rewards are built in, or intrinsic.

MIT's Tom Malone and Stanford's Mark Lepper have outlined seven types of intrinsic motivators.[10] Three of these motivators—competition, cooperation, and recognition—involve interaction among people; they are group-level intrinsic motivators. Because connected products can link people together over time and space, they can leverage group-level intrinsic motivators to influence users.

Competition is perhaps the most powerful group-level intrinsic motivator. When you set up a competition, people become energized; they invest time and effort; they care about the outcome. You don't even need to offer a prize (an extrinsic motivator) to the winner. Not everyone is competitive by nature, but in most situations and for most people, competition is energizing and motivating.

Principles of Mobile Persuasion

Mobile technologies can motivate and influence users by leveraging one or more of the following nine principles.

Kairos Mobile devices are ideally suited to leverage the principle of kairos—offering suggestions at opportune moments—to increase the potential to persuade.

Mobile Loyalty Mobile applications that are perceived to serve the needs and wishes of the owner first, rather than those of an outside party, will have greater persuasive powers.

Mobile Marriage Mobile applications designed to persuade should support an intensive, positive relationship (many interactions or interactions over a long time period) between the user and the product.

Information Quality Computing technology that delivers current and relevant information has greater potential to create attitude or behavior change.

Social Facilitation People are more likely to perform a well-learned target behavior if they know they are being observed via computing technology, or if they can discern via technology that others are performing the behavior along with them.

Social Comparison People will have greater motivation to perform a target behavior if they are given information, via computing technology, about how their performance compares with the performance of others, especially others who are similar to themselves.

Competition Computing technology can motivate users to adopt a target attitude or behavior by leveraging human beings' natural drive to compete.

Cooperation Computing technology can motivate users to adopt a target attitude or behavior by leveraging human beings' natural drive to cooperate.

Recognition By offering public recognition (individual or group), computing technology can increase the likelihood that a person or group will adopt a target attitude or behavior.

Cooperation is another motivator, one that seems to be built into human nature. When people belong to a work group, most of them cooperate. Whenever there is a pressing need, a call for cooperation will naturally motivate most people to help out.

Finally, people are intrinsically motivated by recognition. Many organizations leverage the power of recognition. Employers create "Employee of the Month" awards, blood banks give out "I've donated" stickers for people to wear, and top students get listed on the honor roll. These and many other programs leverage the motivating power of recognition.

In summary, when interactive technologies are networked, they can be designed to use competition, cooperation, and recognition as motivating forces. In this way, connected computing products gain power to persuade.

The Future of Mobile and Connected Persuasive Technology

Today [in 2002], products that are both mobile and connected are scarce. But this will change. In the future we're likely to see a wide range of devices and applications, including those designed to motivate and persuade. The growth will come as mobile phone systems allow people and companies to easily create and deploy applications. While mobile persuasion in the service of mobile commerce will receive lots of attention and funding, a clear win is using mobile technology to help people achieve their own goals. As I see it, mobile persuasion is one of the most promising frontiers in persuasive technology.

Notes and Reference

[1] For an idea of how simple this representation can be, see Social translucence: designing social infrastructures that make collective activity visible, by Thomas Erickson, Christine Halverson, Wendy A. Kellogg, Mark Laff, and Tracee Wolf (IBM T.J. Watson Research Center, Hawthorne, NY). Communications of the ACM, Volume 45, Issue 4 (April 2002). Supporting community and building social capital. ACM Press New York Pp: 40–44.

[2] Roberts, Glyn C., Spink, Kevin S., & Pemberton, Cynthia L. (1999). Learning experiences in sport psychology (2nd ed.) Illinois: Human Kinetics.

[3] Zajonc, R. (1965). Social facilitation, *Science*, 149, 269–274. See also Aiello, J. R., & Douthitt, E. A. (2001). Social facilitation from Triplett to electronic performance monitoring. Group Dynamics: Theory, Research, and Practice, 5(3), 163–180.

For other research on virtual social facilitation, see Aiello, J.R. & Svec, C.M. (1993). Computer monitoring of work performance: Social facilitation and electronic presense. Journal of Applied Social Psychology, 23(7) 537–548. For research on the topic of virtual environments and social influence, including social facilitation, see the work of UC Santa Barbara's James J. Blascovich and colleagues at http://www.psych.ucsb.edu/research/recveb/.

[4] For more about how social influence dynamics can play out virtually, see the work of UC Santa Barbara's James Blascovich. One of his most recent publications is

Blascovich, J. (2002). Social influence within immersive virtual environments. In R. Schroeder (Ed.) The social life of avatars. (pp 127–145). Springer-Verlag.

Web presence: http://www.psych.ucsb.edu/fac/blasc98.htm

[5] For activities that are not well learned, the presence of others will *decrease* performance. In other words, you will do worse when learning a new skill if you know that others are observing you.

[6] Although not directed toward fitness, researchers at IBM have been working on how to use computer technology to virtually represent coworkers who are in a remote location but also working. See

Social translucence: designing social infrastructures that make collective activity visible, by Thomas Erickson, Christine Halverson, Wendy A. Kellogg, Mark Laff, and Tracee Wolf (IBM T.J. Watson Research Center, Hawthorne, NY).

Communications of the ACM, Volume 45, Issue 4 (April 2002). Supporting community and building social capital. ACM Press New York, Pages: 40–44

[7] The IBM researchers use simple circles to represent people in their system. Ibid.

[8] This was first articulated by Festinger, L. (1954). A theory of social comparison process. *Human Relations, 7,* 117–140.

[9] The classic work in social comparison supports the idea that similarity matters. Festinger, L. (1954). A theory of social comparison process. *Human Relations, 7,* 117–140.

A recent discussion (and review) of social comparison and how similarity figures into this process is by

Suls, J., Martin, R., & Wheeler, M. (2002). "Responding to the Social World: Explicit and Implicit Processes in Social Judgments and Decisions." Chapter for Fifth Annual Sydney Symposium of Social Psychology, March 20–22, 2002. Available online at http://www.sydneysymposium.unsw.edu.au/2002/papers/ (click on "Suls chapter").

[10] As described by Malone and Lepper, the seven intrinsic motivators are fantasy, curiosity, challenge, control, competition, cooperation, and recognition. See Malone, T., & Lepper, M. (1987). Making learning fun: A taxonomy of intrinsic motivation for learning. In *Aptitude, Learning, and Instruction* (Eds. R.E. Snow and M.J. Farr). Hillsdale, N.J.: Lawrence Earlbaum.

Acknowledgments

Creating a book requires the cooperation of many people. The book you have in your hands required more than that because we created the whole thing—concept to reality—in less than seven weeks. To pull off this feat, our team went beyond mere cooperation; they made significant personal sacrifices. As editors we are extremely grateful for those sacrifices—and for everyone's cheerful attitudes along the way.

First of all, we thank Nadja Blagojevic. She was our very capable project manager. In our early thinking about this book, we as editors wondered who would manage all the project details and keep everyone on schedule. Neither of us wanted that role. So we asked Nadja. If she had said no we might have scrapped the book project. Or it may have taken months—perhaps years—to complete. Fortunately, Nadja said no to other opportunities and said yes to us. We hope the many phone calls, emails, and long hours coordinating this project bring her many rewards in the future.

Next, we want to thank Jeannine Drew, our consulting editor. Jeannine is usually booked months in advance. Once we started the project, we realized we needed her help immediately if we were going to meet our tight deadline. We are immensely grateful that she agreed to push back some other projects in order to give us a hand. Each chapter—and the collection as a whole—is better because of her keen insight and no-nonsense critiques.

We also appreciate other people who helped us at various stages, all working on tight deadlines and living up to our high expectations. We thank Edward Wade for his eagle eyes on the manuscript. Our appreciation to Yoshimi Munch and Nao Ishitsuka for cover design help. And thanks to our typesetter, Kathy Noverr, for making the pages look good. In addition, we appreciate Eileen Gittens, the CEO of Blurb, who played a special role. We won't go into details, but we'll just say this: Be sure to work with Blurb whenever you can. They deliver.

Of course, we must acknowledge the fast and excellent work of the authors in this volume. Thanks for seeing the vision and changing your schedules to be part of the adventure.

Finally, we each want to thank our closest companions. We saw the sacrifices they made for us day by day. And we realized how much we neglected our personal duties. We promise to make up for this neglect in the future. Perhaps a long trip to Hawaii for the four of us would be nice . . .

B.J. Fogg, Ph.D.
Dean Eckles